# 英語12招行遍天下
## Effective Communication

By Daisie M.T. Chen
Thomas Deneau

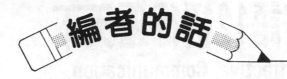

# 編者的話

見到外國朋友時，一般人都會以 " How are you? " 或 " How do you do? " 來問候對方，但對方一句 " Fine, thanks. " 之後，便不知如何接口。您可知美國人偏愛以讚美的方式來當開場白？如果您能適時地來上一句 " *You look nice today.* " ，不僅對方感到驚喜，你們的談話也會很快地熱絡起來。「**英語 12 招行遍天下**」便是針對這種 **日常生活、工作及旅遊**時，可能碰到各種英會場合的突發狀況，提出解決方法，幫助您更有自信開口，無往不利。

「**英語 12 招行遍天下**」內容分兩大部份，第一部份介紹會話可能發生的 **11** 種狀況，告訴您談話開始或結束時，該怎麼說最恰當；在談話中有人偏離主題，或是您漏聽了

別人說的內容時該說什話來彌補；另外當您想插入別的話題、轉移話題，或是彼此產生誤解時又該怎麼表達與澄清等等。第二部份則介紹**表現自我**時的慣用句型 **40** 種，告訴您表達自己有所希求時，除了說 " I want ～ "，還可以較客氣地說 " I would like to ～ " 等。

　　隨著國際化時代的來臨，英語是您趕上潮流的必修課題，說一口流暢的英語，對您交友及工作均有莫大的幫助。而要想**輕鬆地、有效率地**學英語，「**英語 12 招行遍天下**」是您最佳選擇！

　　本書在蒐集資料及編校的過程中，均力求嚴謹，倘有疏漏之處，誠盼各界先進不吝批評指正。

# CONTENTS

## PART I

### 精通口語英會11招

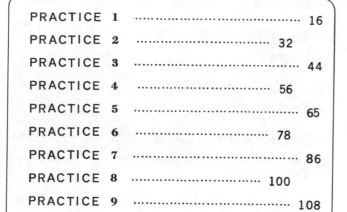

# PART II

## 精通口語英會第12招
## 自我表現句型 40

## Editorial Staff

● 編著／陳美黛

● 校訂

劉　毅・陳瑠琍・黃馨週・張玉玲・鄭明俊

蔡琇瑩・謝靜芳・黃慧玉・施悅文

● 校閱

Thomas Deneau ・ Kevin Caffrey

Dorothy Carin ・ Andrew Hontley

Patrick Bohlein

● 封面設計／張鳳儀

● 版面設計／張鳳儀・白雪嬌

● 版面構成／白雪嬌・周國成

● 打字

黃淑貞・倪秀梅・吳秋香・蘇淑玲

# I

---

# PART

# 精通口語英會11招

11 Ways Of Mastering English
Conversation

# 1

## Excuse me ·······
### 引起對方注意

💭 引起注意的詞語，在英文中稱為 **attention getters** 。要與陌
生人展開談話，最常用的 attention getters 有下面幾種，注
意使用時的語調。

**Sir** ··· （先生～）
**Miss** ··· （小姐～）
**Ma'am** ··· （女士～）

---

A : *Oh, miss* ? ( ⤴ )
B : Yes ? ( ⤴ )

A : I think you dropped this.
B : Oh, did I ? Oh, yes, I did. Thank you.

A : You're welcome.

---

A：噢，小姐。
B：什麼事？

A：我想妳掉了這個。
B：噢，是嗎？是的，謝謝你。

A：不客氣。

A : **Sir**?（ ↗ ）Has the flight to Detroit departed yet?
B : Yes. That flight left ten minutes ago.

A : Can I get a new reservation tonight to Detroit?
B : I'm sorry. We don't have any more flights to Detroit.

A : What about tomorrow?
B : Yes, we have many flights tomorrow.

　　A：先生，往底特律的班機起飛了嗎？
　　B：是的。那個班機十分鐘前起飛了。

　　A：我可不可以重新預訂今晚到底特律的機位？
　　B：很抱歉，沒有前往底特律的班次了。

　　A：那明天呢？
　　B：可以，我們明天有許多班次。

* flight〔flaɪt〕*n.*（飛機的）班次
  depart〔dɪˈpɑrt〕*v.* 離開；出發
  reservation〔ˌrɛzəˈveʃən〕*n.* 預約

🎧 相當於中文「喂！」的說法，有幾個美國人偏愛的口語用法，如下：

　　**Hey, you guys**〔gaɪz〕!
　　**Yoo-hoo**〔ˈjuˈhu〕!
　　**Hey, folks**〔foks〕!

A : **Hey, you guys,** be quiet and start working now.
B : All right.

　　A：嘿，各位，安靜下來開始工作吧！
　　B：好的。

A : ***Yoo-hoo*** !
B : Yeah ?（ ↗ ）

A : Did I get any mail today ?
B : Yes, you did. You have three letters.

A : Thanks.

---

A：喂！
B：幹嘛？

A：今天有没有我的信？
B：有，有三封你的信。

A：謝謝。

\* yoo-hoo〔'ju'hu〕*inter.* 喂（用於引起遠處者的注意時）

---

A : ***Girls*** ! Ballet class will begin now.
B : Where do we put our belongings ?

A : Please put them in the corner.

---

A：各位！芭蕾舞課現在要開始了。
B：我們帶的東西要放在哪裡？

A：請放在角落。

\* ballet〔bæ'le〕*n.* 芭蕾舞
belongings〔br'lɔŋɪŋz〕*n. pl.* 隨身物品

☞ 至於 " Yo " 或 " Hey you "，雖然意思相同，但比較不尊重，
最好少用。

在稍微正式的情況下，應該說相當於中文「對不起～」的話來引起對方注意，常用的說法有下列幾種。

> **(Do you) mind (if)...?**　（你介意～嗎？）
> **Excuse me....**　（對不起～）
> **Pardon〔ˈpɑrdn̩〕me....**　（對不起～）
> **Sorry....**　（抱歉～）

---

A : *Do you mind* ?
B : No... not at all... what can I do for you ?

---

A：你會介意嗎？
B：不，一點也不，我可以為你做什麼？

---

A : *Excuse me, sir.*
B : Are you talking to me ?
A : Yes. Does this bus go cross-town ?
B : No. You need to take the bus across the street.
A : Thank you.
B : You're welcome.

---

A：對不起，先生。
B：你是在和我說話嗎？

A：是的。這班公車有沒有經過市區？
B：沒有。你必須搭對面的公車。

A：謝謝。
B：不客氣。

＊ cross-town〔ˈkrɔsˌtaʊn〕*adv.* 橫越市區

A : ***Excuse me, miss***. Are you Miss Jones ?

B : No, I'm her secretary. May I help you ?

A : Uh, yes. Can I make an appointment to see Miss Jones ?

B : Sure. When would you like to see her ?

A：對不起，小姐。妳是瓊斯小姐嗎？

B：不，我是她的秘書。需要我效勞嗎？

A：是的，我能和瓊斯小姐約個時間見面嗎？

B：當然可以。你想什麼時候見她？

🔊 若認識對方，可用下列方式引起他或她的注意。

**Pardon me, Tom.** （對不起，湯姆。）

**Excuse me, Mary.** （對不起，瑪麗。）

A : ***Excuse me, Mary.*** （ ↗ ）

B : Yeah ? （ ↗ ）

A : Can I borrow your blue dress ?

B : Sure. Just return it right away because I might need it.

A : Thanks a lot.

A：對不起，瑪麗。

B：什麼？

A：可不可以借我妳的藍色洋裝？

B：當然可以。穿完要立刻還我，因爲我可能要穿。

A：非常謝謝妳。

§ 在餐館中需要服務生時，可以直呼其職稱來引起注意。

Waiter〔'wetɚ〕！　　　（服務生！）

Waitress〔'wetrɪs〕！　　（服務生！）

（法）Maître d'〔,metrəˈdi〕！（經理！）

---

" *Waiter*, will you serve the nuts — I mean, would you serve the guests the nuts？"

---

"服務生，你來服侍這些瘋子—— 我是說，可不可以請你拿核桃給這些客人？"

＊ nut〔nʌt〕 *n.* 堅果；核桃；（*pl.*）（俚）瘋子

☞ 這句話的趣味在於" nuts "（核桃）一字，也有「瘋子、怪人」的意思。乍聽之下，會讓人誤以為是「去服侍這些瘋子」，再聽下去，才知是誤解。此乃取其一語雙關的幽默性，令人不覺莞爾一笑。

---

A：*Waitress*！

B：Yes, sir, what can I do for you？

A：I can't eat this stuff. Call the manager！

B：It's no use. He won't eat it, either.

---

A：服務生！

B：是的，先生。要我為您服務嗎？

A：這些東西我實在難以下嚥。去叫你們經理來！

B：沒用的，這些東西他也不會吃的。

A : **Waiter**, there's a dead fly swimming in my soup !
B : Nonsense, ma'am — dead flies can't swim.

　　A：服務生，有隻死蒼蠅在我的湯裏面游泳！
　　B：胡扯，夫人 ——死蒼蠅是不會游泳的。

　* nonsense〔'nɑnsɛns〕*n.* 胡扯

A : **Maître d'**, I have dinner reservations for two in the name of Steve.
B : I am sorry, sir. I don't have your reservation here.
A : I remember making reservations for the Saloon at 8:00 pm.
B : This is not the Saloon, sir. This is the Four Seasons.

　　A：經理，我用史蒂夫的名義預訂了兩個吃晚餐的座位。
　　B：很抱歉，先生。我這裡並沒有登記。
　　A：我明明記得向沙龍餐廳預約今晚八點。
　　B：這裏不是沙龍餐廳，先生，這裏是四季餐廳。

　* maître d'〔,metrə'di〕*n.* (法)餐館經理 ( = *maître d'hôtel* )

🈂 當對方是警官時，亦可以直呼其頭銜或職稱來當禮貌性的招呼語。

　如：

　　　**Officer**〔'ɔfəsə〕, … ( 警官，～ )

　　　**Sir**, …　　　　　　( 先生，～ )

A : *Officer*, would you help me find my cat ?

B : What does it look like ?

A : She is all black, with lots of fur and white fur around the eyes.

B : Give me your phone number. I'll call you if I see her.

A：警官，你能幫我尋找我的貓嗎？

B：牠長什麼樣子？

A：是全黑的，毛很多，在眼睛周圍有一圈白色的毛。

B：留下你的電話號碼。如果找到的話，我會通知你。

* fur〔fɜ〕 *n.* 毛

◎ 日常使用的問候語，加上對方的名字，也是極自然的招呼語。

**Good afternoon, *Mr. Lee*.**（午安，李先生。）

**Good morning, Ms. Hobbs.**（早安，哈伯女士。）

A : *Good afternoon*, *Mr. Lee*.

B : Good afternoon, Sam. What can I do for you ?

A : Just one question, sir. When will you be back from Canada ?

B : Barbara and I will return from there a week after Christmas.

A：午安，李先生。

B：午安，山姆。有事嗎？

A：只有一個問題，閣下。您去加拿大何時回來？

B：我和芭芭拉會在聖誕節後一個禮拜回來。

* Christmas〔'krɪsməs〕 *n.* 聖誕節

A : ***Good Morning, Ms. Hobbs.***
B : Good Morning, Jack !
A : I'm looking forward to working for your company.
B : We are glad to have you.
A : Thank you, Ms. Hobbs. I will see you Monday
　　morning.
B : Yes, see you then, Jack !

　　　A：早安，哈伯女士。
　　　B：早安，傑克。
　　　A：我一直在期待著到你們公司上班。
　　　B：我們很高興能請你來。
　　　A：謝謝，哈伯太太，星期一早上見。
　　　B：好，再見，傑克。

　　＊ ***look forward to*** 期待

Ⓢ 直呼其名最能吸引對方的注意力。

A : ***Jennifer* !**
B : Yeah ?
A : Where have you been ?
B : I was on vacation.
A : Did you have fun ?
B : No, I slept most of the time.

　　　A：珍妮佛！
　　　B：什麼事？
　　　A：妳到哪兒去了？
　　　B：去渡假。
　　　A：玩得高興嗎？
　　　B：不怎麼樣，大部份時間我都在睡覺。

A： *Linda*！

B： Hi. Sam！（ ↗ ）

A： Do you want to go to a party tonight？

B： Where is it being held？

A： At 21 Park Avenue at 11:00 p.m.

B： Sure, I would love to go.

A： Great！ I'll pick you up at 10:30.

---

A：琳達！

B：嗨，山姆！

A：今晚妳要去參加宴會嗎？

B：在哪裏舉行呢？

A：晚上十一點在公園大道21號。

B：當然，我很想去。

A：太棒了！我十點半來接妳。

\* avenue〔ˊævə,nju〕*n.* 大街；大道　　*pick sb. up* 接～；載～

🔗 雙方要展開對話時，先說相當於中文「嗯～」「是這樣～」
「看！」的話，再道出主題（ topic；subject ），可讓對方
注意力集中，完全掌握話題重心。類似說法有：

**Um** …　（嗯～）　　　　　**Well** …　（嗯～）

**So** …　（是這樣～）　　　**Look** …　（瞧！聽！你看！～）

**Listen** …　（聽我說，～）

**Say,** …　（那個，～）（喂，～）

**（You）see** …　（知道嗎？～）

A : *Well* ... I don't know what to say.
B : What is it ?
A : I hope you say "yes." I want to go out with you.
B : Would you give me time to think it over ?
A : Yes, all the time you need.

A：嗯…我不知道該怎麼說。
B：什麼事？
A：我希望妳能答應。我想和妳一起出去。
B：給我時間考慮一下，好嗎？
A：好的，隨便妳考慮多久都可以。

A : *So*! The purpose of this meeting is to reconfirm details for the party.
B : How many people can come ?
A : No more than a hundred.
B : I have more than one hundred confirmed.
A : Uh oh! We have a problem. The hall can not accommodate any more than one hundred people.

A：是這樣的，這次會議的目的是要再確定宴會的一些細節。
B：有多少人能來呢？
A：不能超過一百個。
B：有一百多個人跟我確定說要來。
A：噢！這樣就有問題了。那個大廳容納不下一百多個人。

\* reconfirm〔,rikən'fɜm〕*v.* 再確定　hall〔hɔl〕*n.* 大廳
accommodate〔ə'kɑmə,det〕*v.* 容納

A : *Look*! A woman has lost her luggage.
B : What does it look like?

A : It's red with blue writing on it. Have you seen it?
B : Yes, I have. My husband took it to the lost and found department.

A : Thank you very much.
B : You are welcome.

---

A：瞧，有個女士遺失了她的行李。
B：是什麼樣子的？

A：是紅色的，上面有藍色的字。你看見過嗎？
B：是的。我先生把它拿到失物招領處去了。

A：非常**謝謝**你。
B：不客氣。

* *the lost and found department* 失物招領處

---

A : *Say, Connie*（ ↗ ）.... How are things going?
B : Not bad. I am preparing for school. It starts next week.

A : I know you will do well. Good luck!
B : Thanks, I'll need it.

---

A：喂，康妮…最近好不好呢？
B：還不壞。我正在準備學校的功課，下禮拜就開學了。

A：我知道你一定能應付得很好的。祝妳好運！
B：謝謝，我需要一點好運。

◎ 有時如同中文「注意！」「小心！」的口語，也能為自己製造
一段與人對話的機會。

**Watch out !** （小心！）

---

A : ***Watch out*** !
B : What's the problem ?
A : Here comes a truck !
B : Oh.
A : You should watch where you are going.
B : You're right.  Thanks.

---

　　　A：小心！
　　　B：怎麼了？
　　　A：有輛卡車來了。
　　　B：噢！
　　　A：走路時小心點。
　　　B：你說的對，謝謝。

* truck〔trʌk〕*n.* 卡車

◎ 當對方為不特定的多數時，在會議及會場內的廣播，或是在法
庭上，最常用來喚起他人注意的說法，是相當於中文的「肅靜！」
「注意！」。如：

**Attention**〔əˋtɛnʃən〕**, please !** （請注意！）

**May I have your attention, please ?** （請注意！）

**Order in the court**〔kɔrt〕**!** （法庭上請保持肅靜！）

A : ***Order in the court***!
B : Is the trial beginning now?

A : Yes. Smith versus Jones will begin now. Please take your seat.
B : Can I take photographs in the courtroom?

A : No. No cameras are allowed without permission.

　　A：法庭上請保持肅靜。
　　B：審判要開始了嗎？

　　A：是的，史密斯和瓊斯的案件就要開始審理了，請就位。
　　B：我能在法庭裏拍照嗎？

　　A：不行。未經准許，不得使用照相機。

\* trial〔'traɪəl〕*n.* 審判　　***take one's seat*** 就位
　courtroom〔'kɔrt,rum〕*n.* 法庭
　permission〔pə'mɪʃən〕*n.* 允許

# PRACTICE 1

請根據提示的場合及對象，練習使用最適當的招呼語。

《參考答案：p. 171》

(1) to Professor Brown

A : _____

B : Hi, John. How may I help you?

A : I'm worried about my grades. Would you suggest a tutor?

B : Don't worry. I'll help you.


(2) to a young boy, whose name you know is Tom

A : _____ !

B : Yeah?

A : If you are not careful, you'll hurt yourself.

B : I like playing on the elevator.

A : I know, but if you continue, you'll fall. So, stop it.

B : Okay.


(3) to a stranger at a party

A : _____ Are you Bill Hayes?

B : No, I'm Bill Mayes.

A : I thought it was Hayes.

B : No, it's Mayes. What is your name?

A : Polly.

B : Oh, I thought your name was Holly!

A&B : Anyway, nice to meet you!

(4) to a person at a store

A : _____

B : Yes. May I help you ?

A : Yes. May I speak to the manager of the store ?

B : I am the manager of the store.

A : Good！ I would like to introduce you to a new line of designer dresses.


(5) to your co-worker（同事）, Steve

A : _____

B : Yes ?

A : May I ask you a question ?

B : Sure. I don't mind.

A : Where did you buy that jacket ?


(6) to a receptionist （接待員）

A : _____ Where is the lost and found department（失物招領處）?

B : Go six doors down the hallway. Turn left, and then right. You will see it in front of you.

A : Is there a shorter way to go ?

B : No. I'm afraid not.

# 2 | *May I speak with you?*
## 展開對話

　　我們若已成功地吸引對方的注意，那麼接下來就要「展開對話」了。此時，該使用何種方法來展開對話，要依當時對話的狀況來決定。不過，大致可分為**自我介紹、發問、及狀況的描述**三大類。

🔄 在陌生人群集的聚餐或集會等場合，「自我介紹」是打破僵局（ breaking the ice ），走入人群的第一步。最常以 " **Hello** " 或 " **Hi** " 這一類的招呼語做開頭。

> *Hello*, my name is Steve Wang. I'm a friend of Roger Smith. I'm a reporter for the China Times.

　　您好，我的名字叫史帝夫‧王，我是羅傑‧史密斯的
　　朋友，並且是中國時報的記者。

* *China Times* 中國時報

◎ 如有友人作伴，應一併介紹：

---

A : *Hello, I am Tim Chen. This is my friend Michael Huang.*　I am his interpreter.　He does not speak English.

B : Will he study English in America ?

A : Oh yes ! He has come here for that purpose.

---

A：您好，我是提姆‧陳，這是我的朋友麥可‧黃。
　　我當他的翻譯，他本人不會說英文。

B：他會在美國學英文嗎？

A：噢，是的！他來這裏的目的就是要學英文。

* interpreter 〔ɪn'tɝprɪtɚ〕 *n.* 翻譯員

◎ 若覺得和某些人似曾相識的話，可以使用略帶疑問的語句來展開自我介紹，先報上自己的名字，是尊重對方的表現：

**Haven't we met before ?**　（我們以前見過面嗎？）

**Your face looks familiar** 〔fə'mɪljə〕.（你看起來很面熟。）

---

Excuse me... *haven't we met before* ?　My name is Steve Wang.　You're Bill Johnson, aren't you ? Remember me ?

---

對不起…我們以前見過嗎？我叫史帝夫‧王，你不是
比爾‧強森嗎？還記得我嗎？

A : Sorry to bother you. *Your face looks familiar*.
B : You may have seen me in television commercials.
A : No, that's not it. Weren't you one of my high school students ?
B : Why, yes ! Mrs. Petersen ! I didn't recognize you.

A：很抱歉打擾你，你看起來很面熟。
B：您可能在電視廣告上看過我。

A：不，不是的。你是不是我高中的學生呢？
B：什麼，是的！彼德生太太！我剛沒認出您來。

* commercial〔kə'mɝʃəl〕*n.* 商業廣告
　recognize〔'rɛkəg,naɪz〕*v.* 認得

⑤ 當求職或洽公時打電話，也就是當對方是不認識的人時，需要在電話中自我介紹，應使用 This is～或 My name is～的說法。

**Hello, this is Tom Cheng.** （喂，我是湯姆‧程。）
**Hello！My name is Anita Baker.**
（喂！我叫安妮塔‧貝克。）

*Hello*, *this is Tom Cheng*, a student of Columbia University. I'm calling about your ad for an interpreter.

喂，我是湯姆‧程，哥倫比亞大學的學生。我想請問你們是不是登廣告要徵翻譯員？

* ad〔æd〕*n.* 廣告
　interpreter〔ɪn'tɝprɪtɚ〕*n.* 翻譯員

A : *Hello*！*My name is Anita Baker*. I am responding
   to the job advertisement in the China Post.
B : Yes. Can you come in for an interview on Tuesday?

A : Yes, I can. What time?
B : Please come at 10:30 am. Don't forget your
   résumé.

> A：喂！我叫安妮塔・貝克。我看到了在中國郵報上
>    的徵才廣告，想應徵。
> B：好的。妳能不能星期二過來面談？
>
> A：可以。什麼時間？
> B：請於早上十點三十分來，別忘了帶履歷表。

* respond〔rɪ'spɑnd〕*v.* 回應　interview〔'ɪntə,vju〕*n.* 面談
  résumé〔,rɛzʊ'me〕*n.* 履歷表

🔄 展開對話時，「**發問**」是獲取某些情報的方法，特別是當雙方
的文化背景及經驗不同時。常用的寒喧語是最簡單的「發問」法：

**What's up（with you）?** （你好嗎？／怎麼了？）
**How are you（doing）?** （你好嗎？）
**How do you do?** （你好嗎？）
**What's new?** （你好嗎？／有什麼新鮮的嗎？）
**What's happening?** （你好嗎？／發生了什麼事嗎？）

A : *What's up*？
B : Not much. What's up with you?
A : Nothing.

> A：怎麼了？
> B：沒什麼。你呢？
> A：沒事。

A : ***How are you today***？
B : I'm fine．How are you？
A : Great．Thanks．

　　　A：你好嗎？
　　　B：我很好，你呢？
　　　A：很好，謝謝。

☞ 回答這種寒喧式發問，則可以說：
　　Fine, thanks．And you?（很好，謝謝。你呢？）
　　Not bad．（還不錯。）　　OK．（很好。）
　　Pretty much the same．（差不多。）
　　Great．（很好。）　　　　Not much．（沒什麼。）
　　Nothing new.（沒什麼新鮮事。）　Nothing much.（沒什麼事。）
此外，被問以後，通常應該反問對方，這是談吐的禮貌之一。

A : ***What's happening***？
B : Nothing much．What about you？
A : Not much．But you know what？（ ↗ ）
B : What？（ ↗ ）
A : I got Michael Jackson's new album！
B : That's great！Can I listen to it？
A : Sure．

　　　A：有什麼新鮮事嗎？
　　　B：沒什麼大不了的。你呢？
　　　A：沒什麼，不過你知道嗎？
　　　B：什麼事？
　　　A：我買了麥可‧傑克森的新專輯。
　　　B：真是太棒了。我可以聽嗎？
　　　A：當然可以。

＊ album〔ˈælbəm〕*n.*（歌曲）專輯

A : ***How have you been***？ I heard you were sick.
B : I'm getting better.
A : Please pay attention to your health.
B : Thank you.

　　A：最近如何？聽說你生了一場病。
　　B：現在好多了。
　　A：請多多保重身體。
　　B：謝謝。

　**\* *take care of*** 照顧

⑤ 接下來，我們來看看真正的「發問」場合：包括向陌生人問路，及進入人多的餐廳、速食店、禮堂等。藉著發問來展開彼此的話題，不僅可以獲取資訊（前者），亦可達到社交的目的（後者）。一般的説法是：

*Excuse me.* **How can I get to Columbia University**？
（對不起，請問到哥倫比亞大學該怎麼走？）

*Sorry to bother you,* *but* **would you tell me where the nearest drugstore is**？
（很抱歉打擾你，請問最近的藥房在哪裏？）

*Sorry to interrupt you,* *but* **what is that you are eating**？
（抱歉，打斷你們談話。請問你們正在吃的是什麼東西？）

*Excuse me,* **is anyone sitting here**？
（對不起，這位子有人坐嗎？）

**Is this seat taken**？（這位子有人坐嗎？）

**Hi, do you mind if I sit here**？（嗨，我可以坐這裏嗎？）

**May I join you**？（我能和你們一起坐嗎？）

**\*** interrupt〔͵ɪntəˈrʌpt〕*v.* 打岔；打斷

A : *Hi ! May I join you* ?
B : Sure.

A : Aren't you new here ?
B : Yes, I've just arrived from Taiwan.

A : Oh yeah ? ( ↗ ) I have a lot of friends from Taiwan.

A：嗨！我可以和你一起坐嗎？
B：當然可以。

A：你剛到這裏嗎？
B：是的，我剛從台灣來。

A：噢，眞的？我有很多台灣來的朋友。

A : *May I share this table with you* ?
B : Yes. Let me move my shopping bag.

A : Thanks. Oh, did you go to Macy's ?
B : Yes. They have a big winter sale now.

A : Did you find good clothes on sale ?

A：我可以和你坐同一桌嗎？
B：可以，我移一下我的購物袋。

A：謝謝，噢，你去過梅西斯百貨公司嗎？
B：去過，他們現在正舉行大型冬季特賣。

A：你有沒有看見好的特價服飾？

* *on sale* 拍賣；特價

A : *Excuse me. Is this seat taken* ?
B : Yes, it is. But there is an empty chair. Just pull it over and join us.
A : Thanks. Do you know what the best item on the menu is?
B : Well, the seafood and vegetables are usually very good.
A : That sounds good. Thanks for the suggestion.

A：對不起，這位子有人坐嗎？
B：是的，有人。不過那裏有張椅子，你可以拿過來和我們一起坐。
A：謝謝。你知道菜單上的哪道菜最好嗎？
B：哦，海鮮和蔬菜通常都很不錯。
A：聽起來滿不錯的，多謝你的建議。

* order〔'ɔrdɚ〕*n.* （在餐館的）點菜
　menu〔'mɛnju, 'menju〕*n.* 菜單

❻ 除了自我介紹、發問以外，「描述狀況，抒發感想，再附加問句（ tag question ）」亦是展開對話的良方。例如：眺望風景時，或是觀看運動比賽時，若與對方有共同的經驗，就可以説：

**This train is very crowded**〔'kraʊdɪd〕**, isn't it** ?
（這火車很擠，是不是？）

**That's really a fascinating**〔'fæsn͵etɪŋ〕**view, isn't it** ?
（那風景眞美，是不是？）

**He's a talented**〔'tæləntɪd〕**player, don't you think** ?
（他是一個天才型的選手，你不覺得嗎？）

A : *This train is really crowded, isn't it* ?
B : Yes. The best time to travel on this train is early in the morning or late at night.

A : Can you get a seat at that time ?
B : Yes. You can also see the beautiful scenery outside the window.

A：這火車眞擠，是不是？
B：是啊，搭這火車最好的時間，不是在清晨就是在深夜。

A：那些時候你找得到位子坐嗎？
B：可以，同時你也可以看看窗外美麗的風景。

\* scenery〔'sinərɪ〕*n.* 風景

A : *Beautiful weather, isn't it* ?
B : Yes！ Hope it stays like this until this weekend.

A : Me too. Have a nice day！
B : You too！

A：天氣眞好，是不是？
B：是啊，希望這種好天氣可以持續到週末。

A：我也希望！祝你有個美好的一天！
B：你也一樣！

\* remain〔rɪ'men〕*v.* 持續；依然

和「狀況描述」非常相似的另一種對話方法，就是以讚美對方（ complimenting ）為話題。也就是說，將我們的談話對象，當作狀況描述的對象，並且極力稱讚和他（她）有關的人或事物。這種方法，特別是在美國，廣泛地被使用著。有時候，也有人不直接問對方 How are you?，而以讚美的話來問候對方，如 You look nice（today）.。像這種方法，不僅被稱讚的人心情會很好，而且打從心底就會對你產生一種好感，是一種非常有效的方法。我們來看看下面的例子：

**That's a beautiful sweater you're wearing.**
（你穿的毛衣很好看。）

**I love your jacket. I've been looking for one just like that.**
（我喜歡你的夾克，我也一直在找一件類似的。）

---

A：Hi, Samson.　How are you?

B：Hi, Barbara.　I'm fine.　Is that a new hairstyle?

A：Yes, it is!

B：*It's beautiful*!

A：Thank you.

---

A：嗨，山森，你好嗎？

B：嗨，芭芭拉，我很好。這是妳的新髮型嗎？

A：是呀！

B：很漂亮。

A：謝謝。

---

A : How long have you been in America?

B : About two months. Why do you ask?

A : *You speak English as if it was your native language.*

B : Thank you.

---

A：你在美國待了多久？

B：大概兩個月。爲什麼問我這個？

A：你說英文就像是在說母語般流利。

B：謝謝。

---

🔕 快速展開話題的另一方法，就是直接詢問對方是否方便談話，這種開場白，會令人有鄭重其事之感。

**May I see you for a moment?**（我可以和你談談嗎？）

**May I speak with you?**（我可以和你談話嗎？）

**Can I talk to you for a moment?**（我可以和你談一下嗎？）

**Do you have a minute?**（你有空嗎？）

---

A : *John, may I see you for a moment?*

B : Yes, Miss Graves?

A : Your grades have improved rapidly.

B : I have been studying very hard.

A : Keep up the good work.

---

A：約翰，我能和你談談嗎？

B：可以，葛瑞芙小姐？

A：你的成績進步得很快。

B：我一直很用功。

A：繼續努力。

A : Before you leave, *Karen, can we meet for a few minutes* ?

B : Is it important ?

A : Yes. We need to review the details for the conference.

B : Well, let's go into my office.

---

A：凱倫，在妳離開之前，我們能談一下嗎？

B：有重要的事嗎？

A：是的。我們需要再檢討一下會議的細節。

B：好吧，來我的辦公室談。

* review〔rɪ'vju〕 v. 檢討　　detail〔'ditel〕 n. 細節
  conference〔'kɑnfərəns〕 n. 會議

Ⓢ 在和友人對話的場合，若是要徵求對方的意見，可以誠摯而虛心地說出：

**May I have your opinion**〔ə'pɪnjən〕**?**（我能聽聽你的意見嗎？）

---

A : Excuse me, Paula. *May I have your opinion* ?

B : About what ?

A : How does this tie look with this shirt ?

B : It looks smart / sharp.

---

A：對不起，寶拉。我能聽聽妳的意見嗎？

B：關於哪方面的？

A：這條領帶配這件襯衫怎麼樣？

B：看起來很正點。

◎ 當我們要説一些比較難以啓口的話時，或是緊急的時候，或是有要緊事時，希望對方能讓你直接切入正題時，就可以説：

**I'll come right to the point.**
（我得開門見山地説。）

**Let me give it to you straight**〔stret〕.
（讓我直接了當地告訴你吧！）

◎ 如要單刀直入地詢問他人時，可以説：

**Let me ask you.** （我來問你。）

**May I ask you something ?**
（我能否問你一件事？）

☞ 回答時，可説 " Sure ! " （當然！），或是 " Go ahead. " （請説。）

◎ 在面試或講課時，則可以使用以下的表現方法。

**Let's get started with your professional experience.**
（我們從你的職業經驗開始談吧。）

**I'd like to start with....** （我想從～開始。）

**First, why don't you tell us（me）about....**
（首先，你何不告訴我〔們〕一些有關於～）

---

A : *Please tell me a little about yourself.*
B : What would you like to know?
A : Well, start with your education and then tell me
    your career goals.

---

A：請你自我介紹一下。
B：你想知道哪一方面的事？
A：哦，先談談你的學歷，然後再告訴我你的工作目標。

A : *May I present my academic credentials*?
B : We only accept Harvard graduates.

A : I studied at Harvard for four years.
B : Did you get your degree?

A : No, not yet.
B : Please reapply when you have obtained your degree.

A：你要不要看看我的成績證明書呢？
B：我們只錄取哈佛的畢業生。

A：我在哈佛唸了四年書。
B：拿到學位了嗎？

A：不，還沒。
B：那就請你拿到學位以後再來應徵。

* academic〔͵ækə'dɛmɪk〕*adj.* 學術的
  credentials〔krɪ'dɛnʃəlz〕*n. pl.* 證明書
  reapply〔͵riə'plaɪ〕*v.* 再應徵
  obtain〔əb'ten〕*v.* 取得

## PRACTICE 2

請根據提示，練習使用各種發問及展開會話的方法。

《參考答案：p.171》

(1) At a party

　A : ＿＿＿＿＿＿＿＿＿＿＿＿＿＿＿

　B : Hi! I'm Sam Perkins.

　A : Are you enjoying the party?

　B : Yes. It's really nice.


(2) At an office

　A : ＿＿＿＿＿＿＿＿＿＿＿＿＿＿＿

　B : Hello. I'm sorry I don't remember you.

　A : Excuse me. My name is Joseph. We met at school last year.

　B : Oh yes! You are right. I'm sorry. I have a bad memory.

　A : That's okay. It's good seeing you again.


(3) In a train in the vicinity (附近) of Montreal

　A : ＿＿＿＿＿＿＿＿＿＿＿＿＿＿＿

　B : It's beautiful.

　A : I think you'd like Paris also.

　B : Yes. Actually, I've lived there, and loved it there, too.


(4) In a pub, listening to jazz

　A : ＿＿＿＿＿＿＿＿＿＿＿＿＿＿＿

　B : Yes. Who's your favorite artist?

A : I don't have a favorite. I like jazz featuring saxophone（薩克斯風）players.

B : I like the flute（橫笛）.

(5) At a tourist information desk

A : _____

B : Well, ideally, it is best to have a car.

A : I don't have a car.

B : The next best mode of transportation is the bus. It's inexpensive and fast.

(6) At a bookstore

A : _____

B : What area of film are you interested in?

A : I would like to read about directing.

B : You should read Hollywood Film Directing by Howard M. Smith. We have it in Aisle（走道；排）# 4 .

(7) At a meeting

A : _____

B : Wait！One of the speakers has not arrived.

A : Who is missing?

B : Mr. Sterling.

(8) At a friend's house

A : _____

B : Oh, thank you. You are very kind for saying so.

A : I really mean it.

B : I know. I like them, too.

# 3 Say what?
## 請對方再說一次

　　初學英文者常會有「聽不懂」的情況出現，因應之道決非逃避或裝懂，讓自己錯失與人溝通的機會，而是採「**重覆**」策略，對於彼此間意見之溝通，不到最後關頭，是不可輕言放棄的。

　　「重覆」的情況，可分爲兩種：

　　(A)聽者要求說話者重覆。

　　(B)說者重覆自己說過的話。

　　在(A)中要求重覆的原因，可分爲三類：聽漏了；不明白說者的意圖何在；及聽不懂或是無法理解。

Ⓢ 「聽漏了」的情況下，聽者或許會覺得很抱歉，但是只要説聲
　 " I'm sorry." 或是 "Sorry." 來要求對方重覆説一遍，應該
　 是沒有什麼問題的。例舉如下：

　　　　**I'm sorry, I didn't catch the last point.**
　　　　（很抱歉，最後一點我沒聽清楚。）

　　　　**I'm sorry, would you mind repeating〔rɪ'pitɪŋ〕that?**
　　　　（很抱歉，你可以再說一遍嗎？）

　　　　**Sorry, I missed what you've just said.**
　　　　（很抱歉，你剛剛說的我沒聽到。）

✂ 若對方是自己親近的人的話，只要輕輕地說聲「什麼？」，並且如下一般，將語調抬高，就可以了。

**What did you say?**（ ➚ ）　　　　（你剛剛說什麼？）
**Say what?**（ ➚ ）　　　　　　　（你說什麼？）
**You are going to do what?**（ ➚ ）（你將要做什麼？）

---

A : May I help you?
B : Yes, I'm looking for Mr. Benson.

A : He's in a meeting now. Can I help you?
B : *I'm sorry, what did you say?*（ ➚ ）

A : I said he's in a meeting.
B : Would you tell him Ann Sullivan was here to see him?

A : Yes, I will.

---

A : 我能為妳效勞嗎？
B : 我正在找班森先生。

A : 他現在正在開會。我能幫妳嗎？
B : 很抱歉，你剛剛說什麼？

A : 我說他正在開會。
B : 你可不可以告訴他安‧蘇莉文要見他？

A : 好的，我會告訴他。

＊ *look for* 尋找
　meeting〔'mitɪŋ〕*n.* 集會

A : ***What did you say***? ( ↗ )
B : Never mind. I don't wish to offend you.

A : No, tell me.
B : I want you to go home.

    A : 你剛剛說什麼？
    B : 別介意，我不想惹你生氣。

    A : 我不會生氣，告訴我。
    B : 我要你回家。

＊ offend〔ə'fɛnd〕v. 觸怒

A : You can come on the ski trip next weekend? ( ↗ )
B : Who can come on the ski trip?

A : You!
B : I can't come. I'll be busy.

A : ***Say what***? ( ↗ )
B : I can't come! My company is really busy this season.

    A : 下禮拜的滑雪之旅你能來參加嗎？
    B : 誰能去滑雪之旅啊？

    A : 你！
    B : 我不能去，我會很忙。

    A : 你說什麼？
    B : 我不能去。我們公司這一季實在是太忙了。

＊ ski〔ski〕v. 滑雪

◎ 不明白說話者的意圖何在時，只要如下一般，清清楚楚地告知
　　對方即可。

> **I don't get it.** （我聽不懂。）
>
> **I'm afraid I don't get what you mean.**
> （我恐怕沒聽懂你的意思。）　）

◎ 對於對方所說的話，聽不懂，或是不能理解的時候，應當將不
　　懂的地方，讓對方知道。

> **I don't understand what you are saying.**
> （我不明白你在說些什麼。）
>
> **I'm getting a little confused** 〔kən'fjuzd〕.
> （我有點搞亂了。）
>
> **I don't think I'm following you.**
> （我想我沒聽懂你的話。）
>
> **(Now) I don't know what you're talking about.**
> （我不知道你在說些什麼。）

A : You have been spreading bad rumours about me.
B : *I don't know what you are talking about.*
A : I heard you said I was a lazy student.
B : That is not true!

　　　　A：你一直在散播一些不利於我的謠言。
　　　　B：我不知道你在說些什麼。

　　　　A：我聽說你說我是個懶惰的學生。
　　　　B：沒有那回事！

\* rumour 〔'rumə〕 *n.* 謠言

§ 以下的「要求重覆」表現方法，是最方便、最常被使用的說法。
練習看看，以順暢又自然的語調說出。

What？( ↗ )　　　　　　　　（什麼？）

Huh？( ↗ )　　　　　　　　（嗯？）

Excuse me？( ↗ )　　　　　（對不起？）

Pardon？( ↗ )　　　　　　（你說什麼？）

I beg your pardon？( ↗ )　（請再說一遍？）

Excuse me. I didn't hear you.（對不起，我沒聽見。）

Would you mind repeating〔rɪˈpitɪŋ〕that？( ↗ )
（你可以再說一遍嗎？）

Could you say that again, please？( ↗ )
（請再說一遍，好嗎？）

---

A : Excuse me. Would you tell me how to get to the subway station?

B : Yes. Turn left at the theater over there. Keep going and then turn right at the second set of traffic lights.

A : *I'm sorry, could you repeat that, please*?

B : Yes, left at the theater, then right at the second set of lights.

---

A：對不起，你能告訴我怎麼到地鐵車站去嗎？

B：好，到那家戲院之後左轉，繼續往前走，到第二個紅綠燈時，再往右轉。

A：很抱歉，能不能請你再說一遍？

B：好的。到戲院左轉，第二個紅綠燈右轉。

＊ subway〔ˈsʌb͵we〕n. 地下鐵

A : I'm going home.
B : *What*?!（↗）

A : I'm going home.
B : Why?

A : Because I'm sleepy.

　　A：我要回家了。
　　B：什麼?!

　　A：我要回家了。
　　B：為什麼呢？

　　A：因為我很想睡覺。

若聽不懂的原因，是對方說得太快，或是聲音太小時，那麼我們就要學學下列「要求對方調整說話方式」的技巧。

**Please speak a little more slowly.**
（請你說慢一點。）

**You speak a bit fast. Slow down a little, please.**
（你說得太快了，請說慢一點。）

**I'm sorry I can't hear you. Will you speak a little louder, please?**
（很抱歉，我聽不見你所說的。請你說話大聲一點，好嗎？）

**Would you slow down a little?**
（請你講慢一點好嗎？）

A : *You're talking too fast*.

B : Did you understand anything I said?

A : No. Would you start again?

---

A : 你說得太快了。

B : 你聽懂我所說的嗎?

A : 不懂。再說一次好嗎?

---

A : Where are my glasses?

B : They are here on the table, Grandmother.

A : *Can you speak louder*?

B : They are here on the table!

---

A : 我的眼鏡在哪裏?

B : 就在這桌子上,奶奶。

A : 你講大聲一點好嗎?

B : 在這桌子上!

---

⑤ 反過來說,若對方要求我們「重覆」時,應當怎麼辦?關於這種情況,應對的方法很多,我們舉出幾個較具有代表性的說法。

| I said … | (我是說～) |
| I asked you … | (我要你～) |
| What I said was … | (我說的是～) |
| I was trying to say … | (我想說的是～) |
| I was saying that … | (我說的是～) |

A : What did you say?

B : *I said,* "Do you want some popcorn?"

A : Oh, no thanks.

　　A：你說什麼？

　　B：我說:「你要不要吃些爆米花？」

　　A：噢，不了，謝謝。

＊ popcorn〔'pɑpˏkɔrn〕*n.* 爆米花

A : I don't think I'm following you.

B : *What I am saying is that* everyone has a right
　　to be happy.

A : Yes. I agree with you.

　　A：我想我沒聽懂你所說的。

　　B：我是說每個人都有快樂的權利。

　　A：是的，我有同感。

Ⓢ 在講課時，演說時，或是會話進行一半時，說話者若要重覆自
　己先前說過的話，可以使用以下的表現方法。

　　**As I said before（earlier）**… （就像我先前說的～）

　　**As I told you,** … （正如我告訴過你的～）

　　**Let me repeat what I said earlier.**
　　（我再重覆一遍我先前說過的。）

　　**I would like to repeat the point I made a few
　　minutes ago.**
　　（我想再重述一遍我幾分鐘前所說的要點。）

A : The newspaper said he tried to hurt himself.

B : But the television newscast said he didn't.

A : *As I have said before*, I don't know which medium to believe, television or newspapers.

B : My parents always say to make up our own minds. My mother hates idle gossip.

A : So do I.

A : 報上說他想傷害自己。

B : 但是電視新聞說他没有。

A : 就像我先前說過的，不知道該相信哪種媒體才好，電視還是報紙。

B : 我父母總是說要自己判斷。我母親很討厭没有根據的謠言。

A : 我有同感。

* newscast〔'njuz,kɑst〕*n.* 新聞廣播
  medium〔'midɪəm〕*n.* 媒體　　idle〔'aɪdḷ〕*adj.* 無因的
  gossip〔'gɑsəp〕*n.* 閒話；謠言

⑤ "As I said...." 或是 "As I told you...." 在日常的會話中使用頻繁，say 或 tell 也可以換成 mention 或是 note。而「如前面所説的」這種表現方法，則可以分別使用下列幾種説法。

**As I mentioned before....**　（就像我以前說的~）

**As I noted**〔'notɪd〕**....**　　（正如我說過的~）

**As noted before....**　　　（就像以前說過的~）

**I've told you.**　　　　　（我告訴過你。）

**Didn't I tell you?**　　　　（我沒告訴過你嗎？）

**I've already mentioned it to you.**

（我早就跟你說過了。）

A : Charlie, don't forget to stop by at Kim's Green Market on the way home.
B : For what?
A : *I've told you* … to pick up some fruit and vegetables.
B : Oh, I forgot, but now I remember.

A：查理，回家時別忘了去金姆果菜市場。
B：為什麼？
A：我告訴過你了…去買些水果、蔬菜回來。
B：噢，我忘了，但現在我想起來了。

A : Why don't you go to Tom's store? They carry the most fashionable clothes in town.
B : I didn't know that.
A : *Didn't I tell you before?* And, it's always publicized in the fashion section of the local newspaper.
B : I guess I need to read the paper more.

A：你為什麼不去湯姆的店呢？他們有賣城裏最流行的服飾。
B：我不知道這件事。
A：我沒告訴過你嗎？而且在當地報紙的流行版上也常有廣告。
B：我想我該多看看報紙。

* publicize〔'pʌblɪ,saɪz〕*v.* 宣傳；發表
section〔'sɛkʃən〕*n.* (報紙的) 版
*the paper* 報紙

# PRACTICE 3

請根據示範會話，在空白處填入最適當的「要求重覆」及「重覆」
的表現方法。　　　　　　　　　　　《參考答案：p.171》

(1) A : (i) _____

　　B : What are you confused about ?

　　A : I don't understand your directions to the museum.

　　(ii) _____ ?

　　B : Okay. Take this train to 96th Street, and then
　　　　change to the D train.


(2) A : _____ What are you trying
　　　　to say ?

　　B : The point is that we should start right away.


(3) A : Conductor（車掌）, (i) _____ ?

　　B : Yes. This train has been delayed（誤點）. Please
　　　　transfer to the local train.

　　A : Will that train take me to Penn Station ?

　　B : (ii) _____ ?

　　A : Will that local train go to Penn Station?

　　B : Yes, it will.


(4) A : I'm sorry, _____

　　B : I said, " The movie starts at 3:00 pm. "

(5) A : I don't understand what you are saying.

B : (i)_____ it is important
that you go to the hospital.

A : Do I look ill?

B : No! (ii)_____?
That's where you are supposed to meet your sister!


(6) A : Hi! My name is Perry.

B : Did you say Terry?

A : _____


(7) A : _____

B : Is it necessary to review (重覆) it again.

A : Yes, in case someone does not understand or did
not hear the instructions.

B : All right.

# 4 Are you saying that?
## 確認對方語意

　　當使用「重覆」及「明瞭化」策略，來逐漸了解對方所說的話時，若覺得自己仍缺乏自信，應該怎麼辦呢？對於平常所聽到的，總覺得自己好像懂了，應當怎樣來確定自己是真的了解了呢？

Ⓢ 當自己一知半解時，不要裝懂，使用以下的「理解的確認」策略，向對方說明。

**If I understand you correctly** 〔kəˊrektlɪ〕**, you mean....**
（如果我沒聽錯的話，你的意思是～）

**Do you mean to tell me....?**
（你的意思是要告訴我～？）

**Let me see if I understand you.**
（讓我想想我是否明白你的意思。）

**You mean.... Am I correct?**
（你是指～，沒錯吧？）

**I'm not sure I follow you. Are you saying that...?**
（我不確定自己是否聽懂你的意思了。你是不是說～？）

A : *If I understand you correctly, you mean* you are
　　against him.

B : Yes, but it isn't personal, just business.

A : So, do you like him as a person?

B : Well, I don't know him very well.

A : You see him only as a business competitor. Am
　　I correct?

B : Yes, that's right.

A：如果我沒會錯意，你是說你反對他囉！

B：是的，但不是個人因素，純屬公事。

A：那麼，他本人你喜歡嗎？

B：嗯，我和他並不熟。

A：你只是把他當做事業上的競爭對手，是嗎？

B：是的，沒錯。

* competitor〔kəmˈpɛtətɚ〕 *n.* 競爭對手

A : *Let me see if I understand you.* I should read
　　Chaucer, Shakespeare and Arthur Miller in
　　order to prepare for the final exam.

B : That's right. Don't forget Hemingway.

A : Let me add his name to my list. So, it's
　　Chaucer, Shakespeare, A. Miller and Hemingway.

B : Right! Now you're all set.

A：讓我想想看自己是否聽懂你的意思。爲了準備期末考，我該唸喬叟、莎士比亞和亞瑟・米勒，是嗎？

B：沒錯，別忘了還有海明威。

A：讓我再把他列入名單裏。所以就是喬叟、莎士比亞、米勒和海明威。

B：對了，現在你已經準備就緒了。

＊ Chaucer〔'tʃɔsɚ〕*n.*喬叟
　（ Geoffrey，英國第一位詩人，著有" Canterbury Tales "）
　Shakespeare〔'ʃek,spɪr〕*n.*莎士比亞
　（ William，1564-1616，英國詩人，戲劇家）
　Arthur Miller 亞瑟・米勒（ 美國劇作家 ）
　Hemingway〔'hɛmɪŋ,we〕*n.*海明威（ Ernest，美國小說家 ）

Ⓢ 不太相信對方説的話時，可以用下列略帶驚訝的「反問」語氣來進行確認。

**You mean John F. Kennedy?**（ ↗ ）　　（你是指約翰・甘迺廸？）
**(Are)you sure that's correct?**（ ↗ ）（你確定是那樣沒錯？）
**Are you sure?**（ ↗ ）　　　　　　　（你確定？）

　＊ John F. Kennedy 約翰・甘迺廸（ 1917～1963，美國第卅五任總統)

A：When will students begin to sign-up for classes?
B：*You mean* " When can students register for school?"

A：學生們何時才開始登記上課？
B：你是說：「學生們何時才能註冊入學」嗎？

＊ *sign-up* 登記　　register〔'rɛdʒɪstɚ〕*v.*登記；註冊

A : *Do you mean to tell me* not to worry？

B : Yes. There is nothing to worry about.
Everything is taken care of.

A : *You mean* you got money for the bills？( ↗ )

B : That's right！

　　A : 你的意思是要叫我不要擔心？

　　B : 是的，沒有必要嘛！事情都處理好了。

　　A : 你是說有錢付帳單了？

　　B : 沒錯！

　* *take care of* 處理　　bill〔bɪl〕*n.* 帳單

A : When will students begin to sign-up for classes？

B : They can register for school today, *if that's
what you mean.*

　　A : 學生們何時才開始登記上課？

　　B : 他們今天就可以註冊入學，如果你指的是這件事
　　　　的話。

Ⓢ 若能站在說話者的立場，一邊進行談話，一邊對於對方是否理
解，來進行確認的話，相信誤會產生之可能性也會隨之減少。
當我們對對方有所要求時，想要確定此一訊息是否已傳達到，
可以使用以下的表現方法。

**Have you got all that？**（你全都聽到了吧？）

**（You）got it？**　　　　（知道了嗎？）

**See？**　　　　　　　　（知道了嗎？）

**OK？**　　　　　　　　（知道了嗎？／好了嗎？）

**Understand？**　　　　　（知道了嗎？）

---

A : Betty, It's important that you finish typing the letter to Mr. Banks by 3:00 p.m. And, please express-mail it to him by 4:00 p.m. *Okay*?

B : I got it. I'll mail it to Mr. Banks by 4:00 p.m.

A : Right.

---

A : 貝蒂，這件事很重要。妳一定要在下午三點前，打完那封要寄給班克斯先生的信。而且請妳在下午四點前，以限時專送寄給他，知道了嗎？

B : 知道了！我下午四點以前會寄給班克斯先生。

A : 好！

\* p.m.〔ˈpiˈɛm〕午後 ( 的 )
express-mail〔ɪkˈsprɛs‚mel〕v. 限時專送
*I got it*！（口語）知道了！

🔉 自己在說明某些複雜的事情時，可以使用以下幾種表現方法，來對於對方的理解進行確認。

**Is what I'm saying clear（enough）?**
（我說的都夠清楚了嗎？）

**Do you follow me?**　　（你懂了嗎？）

**（Are）you with me?**　（你知道我說什麼嗎？）

**Is that clear?**　　　（聽清楚了嗎？）

**Am I clear?**　　　　（我說的夠清楚嗎？）

**You know what I mean?**（你懂我的意思嗎？）

---

A : How was the fashion show?

B : Beautiful! The clothes were so unique. It was just indescribable. *You know what I mean*?（↗）

A : I think so.

B : Yeah. I can't describe them in words.

---

A：那場時裝秀如何？

B：眞是太美了！那些服裝眞的很獨特，實在是難以形容。你知道我的意思吧？

A：大概知道吧！

B：嗯，眞是無法用言語來形容。

* indescribable〔,ɪndɪˈskraɪbəbḷ〕*adj.* 難以形容的
　describe〔dɪˈskraɪb〕*v.* 描述

ⓢ「誤解」對於學習英文的人來說，是個嚴重的問題。雙方的對話，自始至終都在於彼此「意見」之溝通上，因此，有誤會產生時，須積極地去排解。遇到這種情形時，有以下的表現方法。

**I think you have misunderstood me.**
（我想你誤會我的意思了。）

**You may have misunderstood me.**
（你一定誤解我了。）

**It seems that there has been a misunderstanding.**
（似乎有誤會存在。）

**Perhaps we've misunderstood each other.**
（也許我們誤會對方了。）

* misunderstand〔,mɪsʌndəˈstænd〕*v.* 誤會

A : Why can't I wear this dress?

B : Don't take it personally, but this dress is not appropriate for a formal occasion.

A : Why? Do you think it's ugly?

B : No. *I think you've misunderstood me*. You can only wear long formal gowns for the senior prom. Do you understand?

A : Yes, I understand.

　A：為什麼我不能穿這件衣服？

　B：妳不要從自己的角度來想，只是這件衣服不適合正式的場合。

　A：為什麼呢？你覺得這衣服很醜嗎？

　B：不是，我想妳是誤會我了，要參加大四畢業舞會，只能穿長的，正式的晚禮服。知道嗎？

　A：是的，我知道了。

\* appropriate〔ə'propriit〕*adj.* 適合的
　gown〔gaʊn〕*n.* 晚禮服
　prom〔prɑm〕*n.* (大學等所舉行的) 舞會

🔊 由對方的反應，我們明顯地感覺到自己被誤解時，應該如何呢？首先，就先向他說清楚「不要誤會我」，然後，再接著補充說明「我所說的並非如此」。

**Please don't misunderstand me**. (請不要誤解我。)

**Don't get me wrong**. (不要誤會我。)

**I don't want you to get the wrong idea about this**. (我不想讓你誤解這件事。)

**Don't take it personally**. (不要以個人的觀點來想。)

That's not what I meant. （我不是那個意思。）
I'm not saying that. （我沒這麼說。）
I didn't say that. （我沒說過。）
I didn't mean to.... （我並不是要～）
I didn't mean that. （我不是那個意思。）

A : I'm really angry with you.
B : Why? What did I do?

A : You said I was not to be trusted.
B : *Don't get me wrong. That's not what I said.*

A : What did you say?
B : What I said was your car had rusted.

　　A : 你真令我生氣。
　　B : 為什麼呢？我做了什麼嗎？

　　A : 你說我不值得信任。
　　B : 不要誤會我，我沒說過那種話。

　　A : 那你是怎麼說的？
　　B : 我只是說你的車子生銹了。

＊ rust〔rʌst〕v. 生銹

🖎 要排解誤會的下一個步驟就是「說明」。自己想要說明某事時，
可以在說明前，加上一段如下的前言。

　　Let me explain. （聽我解釋。）
　　Allow me to explain. （讓我解釋。）
　　Let me amend my remarks. （讓我修正我所說的話。）

**I'm saying that**....　　（我是說～）

**What I really mean is**....　（我真正的意思是～）

**What I really meant was**....（我真正的意思是～）

🔊 由於第三者介入而產生誤會，使自己成了此項錯誤訊息之被害者時，應該如何呢？此時，如同「我被誤會了」這一類的話，有以下幾種說法。

**I was misinterpreted.**

**I was misquoted.**

**I was misunderstood.**

\* misinterpret〔ˌmɪsɪnˈtɝprɪt, ˌmɪsn-〕*v.* 誤解

misquote〔mɪsˈkwot〕*v.* 誤引用

---

A : Rose told me what you said to her.

B : What did she say?

A : She said you told her that my car was a piece of junk.

B : I didn't say that. I said your car had rusted. *I guess I was misquoted.*

---

A：蘿絲把你跟她說的話都告訴我了。

B：她說了些什麼？

A：她說妳跟她說我的車是一堆廢鐵。

B：我沒這麼說，我是說你的車生銹了。我想我的話被誤引了。

\* junk〔dʒʌŋk〕*n.* 破銅爛鐵

A : Ms. Moviestar, we read in the National Talker that you didn't speak with your fellow actors on the set.

B : *That magazine misinterpreted what I said.* It is true that I didn't speak with the other actors. It is because I played a deaf-mute. So during the filming, I couldn't speak to anyone.

A : I understand. That sheds light on the situation.

　　A : 明星小姐，我們在「國家報導」上看到說，妳在拍片現場不和其他的演員說話。

　　B : 那本雜誌誤解我的話了。我沒和其他演員說話，那是真的。因為我演的是位聾啞的人，所以在拍片期間，我不能和任何人說話。

　　A : 我了解，這樣誤會就澄清了。

* deaf-mute〔'dɛf'mjut〕*n.* 聾啞者
 *shed light on* (喻)澄清；發出光

# PRACTICE 4

請在空白處，試著填入最適當之「理解確認」表現方法。

《 參考答案：p.172 》

(1) A : (i) _____ Would you repeat ?

B : Turn left at the next traffic light. Keep going straight until the fork (叉路) in the road. Then veer (轉向) to the right, and go two blocks until you come to the Bridge. (ii) _____ ?

A : Yes. (iii) _____ going that way will get me to the Golden Gate Bridge ?

B : Yes. Just follow my directions.

(2) A : Mr. Smith, thank you for meeting me today.

B : My pleasure.

A : I wanted to ask you about a statement you made during the last interview.

B : Yes. What is it ?

A : You said you would never seek political office. (i) _____ under no circumstances will you ever enter politics ?

B : Well, if an opportunity presented itself, of course, I would not ignore it. (ii) _____ I will not seek political office this year.

(3) A : Are you coming on the 6:00 p.m. bus?

B : No, I'm coming on the 7:00 p.m. bus?

A : _____? I thought you said 6:00 p.m.

B : I did, but my plans have changed.

(4) A : Senator（参議員）, you are quoted as saying that "All rich people should never go to war."

B : (i) _____. (ii) _____, "People should never go to war."

# 5 What does that mean?

## 打破沙鍋問到底

　　對於擁有不同文化背景的雙方，在進行溝通時，聽不懂雙方的話是常有的事，即使只是一個單字不懂，也可能會錯全意。此時，若礙於面子而裝懂，不但犯了溝通的大忌，變得雞同鴨講，且自己也會白白錯失精進英文能力的大好機會。

　　本章介紹「明瞭化」策略，便是一種打破沙鍋問到底的會話手法，也是提昇英文聽與說能力的捷徑。

⑨ 當不懂對方使用的語句時，應馬上探詢該句話的真正意思，說法有下列幾種。（X 的位置可套用任何字句）

**What does X mean?**　　　　（「X」是什麼意思？）

**What is the meaning of X?**　（「X」是什麼意思？）

**What do you mean by X?**　　（你所謂的「X」是什麼意思？）

**How do you define X as the term being used there?**
（那裏所用的 X，你是如何定義的？）

\* define〔dɪˈfaɪn〕*v.* 定義

A : Mom, *what does " police " mean*?

B : " Police " means a person who protects us. Do you see that man over there? He's a policeman.

A : Can a "policeman" be a woman?

B : Oh yes. They can be police officers, too.

---

A：媽，「警察」是什麼意思？

B：「警察」就是保護我們的人。妳看見那邊那個人嗎？他就是警察。

A：警察可以是個女人嗎？

B：可以，她們也可以成爲警官。

\* protect〔prəˈtɛkt〕*v.* 保護　　***police officer*** 警官

---

A : Are you in a Master's degree program?

B : No. I'm in a Ph. D. program. I'm now working on my dissertation.

A : *What disser … something*?

B : Dissertation. It's a doctoral thesis.

---

A：你在修碩士嗎？

B：不，我修博士，現在正在寫論文。

A：什麼是論…論什麼？

B：論文，是博士論文。

\* ***Master's degree*** 碩士學位

Ph. D. 博士學位（= *Doctor of Philosophy* ）

dissertation〔ˌdɪsəˈteʃən〕*n.* （學位）論文

doctoral〔ˈdɑktərəl〕*adj.* 博士的　　thesis〔ˈθisɪs〕*n.* 論文

§ 需要對方給自己一個具體的說明時，可以請他提出例子及說明。
這種說法，在中文裏，相當於「例如什麼呢？」「可不可以請
你舉例說明呢？」等，在英文中，則有以下的用法。

**Would you give me an example?**
（你能舉個例子嗎？）

**Can you give me an example?** （你能舉例嗎？）

**For example?** （例如？）

**For instance?** （例如？）

**Like what?** （像什麼？）

---

A: Some people like to use big words.

B: *For instance*? ( ↗ )

A: For example, " loquacious." She is very loquacious. Loquacious means talkative.

B: What's wrong with using big words?

A: Nothing. But it is better to use simple words
so that you are easily understood.

---

A: 有些人喜歡用些比較難的字。
B: 像什麼字呢？

A: 例如「饒舌」，她很饒舌。饒舌就是愛說話。
B: 用難字有什麼不好呢？

A: 也沒什麼。不過最好是用簡單的字，這樣別人比
較能聽得懂。

---

\* loquacious 〔loˊkweʃəs〕 *adj.* 饒舌的；多嘴的
talkative 〔ˊtɔkətɪv〕 *adj.* 饒舌的；愛說話的

🔊 以下的幾種說法，是「可不可以請你再說詳細一點呢？」之種
　種表現方法，可供各位參考。

**Would you be more specific**？（你能再說得明確一點嗎？）

**Would you give me a few more details on that**？
（關於那件事，你可以再多告訴我一些細節嗎？）

**Would you please elaborate**？（請你詳細說明，好嗎？）

**Can you elaborate on that**？
（關於那一點，你能詳細說明嗎？）

**Can you explain**〔ɪkˈsplɛn〕**that in detail**？
（你能詳細地解釋那件事嗎？）

**Would you give me a detailed explanation of** …？
（你能給我一個有關～的詳細說明嗎？）

**Would you give me a little more detailed information
about** …？（關於～你能給我比較詳細的資料嗎？）

\* elaborate〔ɪˈlæbə͵ret, ɪˈlæbərɪt〕*v., adj.* 詳細說明（的）

---

A : May I help you, miss？

B : Yes, you may. I need to buy a dress.

A : We have many dresses in this store. What type
　　of dress do you want？

B : I want a blue dress.

A : *Could you be more specific* as to what " type "
　　of dress you prefer？

---

　A： 我能為妳效勞嗎？小姐。

　B： 是的，我想買一件洋裝。

　A： 我們店裏有很多洋裝。妳想要哪一種款式的？

　B： 我要一件藍色的洋裝。

　A： 請妳更明確地說明，妳要的是哪種款式，好嗎？

🕲 當我們不知道對方的語意何在時，除了可仿效前述的幾種說法外，下列的「明瞭化」用法，也是極常用。

> **What does that mean？** （那是什麼意思？）
> **What do you mean by that？**（你那樣說是什麼意思？）
> **What do you mean？** （你是什麼意思？）

---

A： There's something strange about that house.

B： ***What do you mean？***

A： Everytime I walk past, I feel strange.

B： Do you believe in ghosts？

A： Well, I have never seen a ghost. I don't know.
I just feel weird.

B： Maybe we should investigate the house.

A： You can investigate the house alone！ I'm not
going in there.

---

A：那房子有點怪。

B：你這句話是什麼意思呢？

A：每次我走過都會覺得怪怪的。

B：你相信有鬼嗎？

A：哦，我是沒見過鬼。我不知道，我只是覺得有點
怪異。

B：也許我們該查看一下那屋子。

A：你還是自己去查吧！我才不想進去呢！

* weird〔wɪrd〕*adj.* 怪異的
investigate〔ɪn'vɛstə,get〕*v.* 查看

◎ 不明白對方到底在説什麼，為何要這麼説時，直接詢問對方真正的含意，這也是方法之一。但是，這種表現方法，間接上有一種「對於你所説的，我很難贊同」的語氣，因此，在使用上應當特別注意。

**Why do you say that?**（你為什麼這麼説？）

**Why is that?**　　（為什麼會這樣？）

**Why?**　　　　　（為什麼呢？）

---

A: I think Ann is angry with me.

B: ***Why do you say that?***

A: She never speaks to me anymore.

B: That is no reason. Maybe Ann is having problems.

A: I will call her to see if I can help.

---

　　A: 我想安一定在生我的氣。

　　B: 為什麼這麼説呢？

　　A: 她已經不再和我説話了。

　　B: 真沒道理，也許安面臨了什麼問題。

　　A: 我會打電話給她，看看能不能幫得上忙。

---

A: I shouldn't have had that coffee.

B: ***Why?*** Was anything wrong with that coffee?

A: I forgot that caffeine gives me headaches.

---

　　A: 我真不該喝那杯咖啡的。

　　B: 為什麼呢？咖啡裏有問題嗎？

　　A: 我忘了咖啡因會使我頭痛。

* caffeine〔ˈkæfiɪn, ˈkæfin〕*n.* 咖啡因

A : Pardon me. Please do not allow your children to feed the animals.

B : *Why not*?

A : It is against the policy of the zoo. If I speak to your children again, your family will have to leave the zoo.

B : We apologize. We will watch our children.

A：對不起。請不要讓你們的小孩餵那些動物吃東西。

B：為什麼不可以呢？

A：這樣做違反了動物園的規定。如果讓我再說一次的話，你們全家就得離開動物園了。

B：很抱歉，我們會注意小孩的。

* feed〔fid〕*v.* 餵
  apologize〔ə'pɑlə,dʒaɪz〕*v.* 道歉

# PRACTICE 5

請試著依劃線部份句意，換其他表「詢問」說法。

《參考答案：p.172》

(1) A : I want a blue dress.

B : <u>Could you be more specific as to what type of dress you prefer</u>?

A : <u>What do you mean by " type "</u>?

B : Well, do you want a wedding, business or party dress ?

A : I see what you mean. I want to buy a party dress.

B : Please follow me. I will take you to our party dress section.

(2) A : As President of the United States, I will eliminate
（消除）poverty and crime.

B : <u>Would you give details on how you will do that</u>?

A : I will be glad to. In fact, here is a booklet (小冊子) outlining my program to eliminate poverty and crime.

(3) A : That American company is building a new plant here.

B : <u>What does " plant " mean</u>?

A : It's a factory.

(4) A : There are different religions practiced in China.

B : <u>Would you give me examples</u>?

A : Buddhism, Taoism and Christianity.

(5) A : Did you see that woman's baby ?

B : No. <u>Why</u> ?

A : The baby has lovely brown eyes.

B : Oh yes. I see them now. They are beautiful !


(6) A : What did you mean by that ?

B : <u>I meant that</u> it is better to be around pleasant people.

A : Do you mean I'm unpleasant ?

B : No! But some people are.

# 6

## In my opinion,…
### 表達自己的意見

　　在會話中，應不斷地陳述自己的意見，使彼此的談話有意義並有內容。然而，若直言不諱地發表自我主張，會給對方一種盛氣凌人的感覺，故高明的「陳述個人意見」方法必須掌握，而這也是本章重心所在。

◎ 首先，最簡單也最常用的，有下列幾種說法。

| I think … | （我想～） | I believe … | （我相信～） |
|---|---|---|---|
| I guess … | （我猜～） | I assume … | （我相信～） |
| I suppose … | （我想～） | It seems to me … | （我覺得～） |

　＊ assume〔ə'sjum〕v. 相信；假設

---

A : I don't know how this Presidential election is going to turn out.

B : *I think* Jeff is going to win. Not that I want him to, but *I guess* he has been pretty successful in his campaigns.

A : *I guess* you are right. *I suppose* he will be the next President.

A：我不知道總統大選的結果會是如何。

B：我想傑夫會當選。不是我希望他當選，而是我想他這次競選活動辦得相當成功。

A：我想你是對的。我覺得他將會是下一任美國總統。

* ***turn out*** 結果　　campaign〔kæm'pen〕*n.* 活動
　suppose〔sə'poz〕*v.* 認為

§ 不太肯定自己的見解是否正確時，或是想要謙虛一點的情況下，可以先說「或許我錯了吧！」「據我所知」「我所聽到的是～」「若我沒錯的話～」等等這一類的話，再陳述自己的意見。

**I may be wrong, but** … ( 我也許是錯的，但是～ )

**As far as I know,** … ( 據我所知～ )

**From what I′ve heard,** … ( 我聽說～ )

**If I am correct,** … ( 如果沒錯的話～ )

**If I understand it (you) correctly,** … ( 如果我沒聽錯～ )

§ 要避免一些比較強硬的說法時，採取「模稜兩可」(hedging) 的策略即可。它就相當於中文的「總覺得～」「大概就是～」等等說法，在英文中，有以下幾種說法。

… **sort**〔sɔrt〕**of** … ( …有點，頗，蠻～ )

… **kind of** … 　　　( …有點～ )

… **in a way** … 　　　( …有點～ )

… **in a sense** … 　　( …有點～ )

*I* **sort of** *like it.* 　( 我蠻喜歡的。)

*That's nice* **in a way.** ( 那東西還不錯。)

*I* **kind of** *want it.* 　( 我有點想要。)

§ 「模稜兩可」的表現方法，用於批評對方或第三者時，或是要說一些難聽的話時，都相當好用。

*He* **sort of** *bothers me.*（我覺得他變煩的。）

*I'm* **kind of** *angry at his behavior.*
（對於他的行為，我覺得有點生氣。）

*My husband* **sort of** *never helps me with anything.*
（我的丈夫好像從來都不會幫我做事。）

* bother〔'baðɚ〕 *v.* 煩擾
  behavior〔bɪ'hevjɚ〕 *n.* 行為

---

A : What's wrong, Kevin?

B : Uh … nothing.

A : Did something happen at school?

B : Well … I can't tell you.

A : Did one of your classmates hurt your feelings?

B : Not just one … John and Bill are *sort of* always picking on me.

A : How terrible! Don't worry, Kevin. I will talk to your teacher tomorrow.

---

A：你怎麼了，凱文？

B：嗯…沒事。

A：在學校發生了什麼事嗎？

B：哦…我不能跟妳說。

A：是不是哪個同學讓你覺得不愉快？

B：不只一個…約翰和比爾似乎總是在批評我。

A：多可怕！別擔心，凱文，明天我會跟你的老師說。

* *pick on* 批評　　terrible〔'tɛrəbḷ〕 *adj.* 可怕的

◎ 以下是特別強調個人見解的方法，也就是在一開頭說「就我個人意見而言」之類的話。

**For me,** … （對我而言，～）

**As I see it,** …（以我看來，～）

**From my personal point of view,** …
（從我個人的觀點看來，～）

**In my opinion,** … （據我的看法，～）

**Personally,** … （以個人而言，～）

**My feeling is that** … （我覺得～）

**I have an impression that** … （我有種想法，就是～）

* *point of view* 觀點
  impression〔ɪmˈprɛʃən〕*n.* 想法

---

A : How was Linda?

B : Not good. She has been having many problems
   since she left home.

A : I know. I'm really worried about her.

B : Me too! *From my personal point of view,*
   I think she should return home.

---

A：琳達還好吧？

B：不怎麼好，從她離家之後，就問題不斷。

A：我知道，我真擔心她。

B：我也是啊！我個人認為她應該回家。

* worry〔ˈwɝɪ〕*v.* 擔心

◎ 想要率直地表達自己的想法時，應該如何呢？可以在一開頭就
　說「老實說」或「說真的」之類的話。

> **Frankly (speaking),** ⋯
>
> **Honestly,** ⋯
>
> **To be frank,** ⋯
>
> **To be honest (with you),** ⋯
>
> **To tell you the truth,** ⋯
>
> **To put it bluntly,** ⋯

> ＊ frankly〔'fræŋklɪ〕*adv*. 坦白地
>
> 　honestly〔'ɑnɪstlɪ〕*adv*. 誠實地
>
> 　bluntly〔'blʌntlɪ〕*adv*. 坦白地

---

A : Howard, how do you like my new dress?

B : Do you want my honest opinion?

A : Well, of course.

B : ***To put it bluntly***, I hate it. It makes you look much older.

---

　　A : 荷華，你覺得我的新衣如何？

　　B : 妳要聽我說實話嗎？

　　A : 哦，當然囉！

　　B : 坦白說，我討厭那件衣服，它讓妳看來老很多。

＊ opinion〔ə'pɪnjən〕*n*. 見解

　***of course*** 當然

　hate〔het〕*v*. 討厭

Ⓢ 英美人士説話時，會傾向於先陳述一般事情的狀況（一般化 generalizing），接著再將實際的事套入説明（個別化 specifying）。而在英文中，表現「一般化」的説法很多，像「一般來説」這類的説法，較常用的有以下幾種：

> **Generally（ speaking ),** …
> **In general**〔'dʒɛnərəl〕, …
> **As a rule,** …
> **By and large,** …
> **In many cases,** …
> **On the whole**〔hol〕, …
> **On the average**〔'ævərɪdʒ〕, …

---

A : Are all Americans rich?

B : Well, *generally speaking*, a small percentage of Americans are considered rich.

A : Are there more middle or lower income Americans?

B : I'd say Americans with middle incomes are in the majority.

---

A：所有美國人都有錢嗎？

B：嗯，一般説來，只有少部分的美國人被認爲有錢。

A：中產或低收入的美國人較多嗎？

B：我會説中產階級的美國人佔大多數。

\* percentage〔pə'sɛntɪdʒ〕 *n.* 百分比
middle〔'mɪdl̩〕 *adj.* 中間的
income〔'ɪn,kʌm, 'ɪŋ,kʌm〕 *n.* 收入
majority〔mə'dʒɔrətɪ〕 *n.* 大半

🔊 「個別化」或是「具體化」的策略，則有以下的表現方法。

  **More specifically**〔spɪˋsɪfɪklɪ〕…（明確一點地說～）
  **To be more specific** …  （具體一點來說～）
  **Here is a specific case** … （這是個特別的案例～）
  **For instance** …    （例如～）

---

My presentation so far has been concerned with how a foreign language is learned. ***More specifically***, I have discussed what affective factors come into play in learning a foreign language.

到目前為止，我的演說是關於如何學外語，明確一點說，我已經討論過，在學外語時，會有哪些情感因素造成影響。

 * presentation〔͵prɛznˋteʃən〕 *n.* 演說
  affective〔əˋfɛktɪv〕 *adj.* 情感的
  factor〔ˋfæktɚ〕 *n.* 因素　　***come into play*** 造成影響

---

A： I don't like Jack.　He is just too confident.
B： Too confident？
A： ***To be more specific***, he is too proud, too proud to learn things from others.

  A：我不喜歡傑克，他就是太有自信了。
  B：太有自信？
  A：具體一點來說，他太傲了，傲得不願跟別人學。

⑤ 有時，爲了陳述自己的意見，便不得不推翻對方的論調。然而，要與對手唱反調，真不是一件簡單的事。我們可以在討論之中，反覆地闡明自己的論點，這也不失爲一個好方法。反駁的方法有二種：(a)直接反駁。(b)有彈性地間接反駁。

(a)的方法，有以下幾種說法。(有的說法相當嚴厲，請注意使用。)

| | |
|---|---|
| **I don't think so.** | ( 我不這樣認爲。) |
| **No, you're wrong!** | ( 不，你錯了！) |
| **That is not true.** | ( 那不是眞的。) |
| **No way!** | ( 絕不！) |
| **I have to disagree with you.** | ( 我不同意你說的。) |
| **I can't agree with you.** | ( 我無法贊同你的看法。) |
| **Oh, no.** | ( 哦，不。) |
| **On the contrary, …** | ( 相反地，～) |

---

A : She is so high-spirited.
B : *I don't think so.*

A : What do you mean?
B : I think it's just an act.

A : I think you are wrong.
B : Maybe. It's a matter of opinion.

---

A：她的精神眞好。
B：我不這樣認爲。

A：你什麼意思？
B：我認爲那只是演戲罷了。

A：我覺得你錯了。
B：或許吧！這只是個人看法不同罷了。

\* high-spirited〔'haɪˌspɪrɪtɪd〕*adj*. 精神好的

⑤ 另外，堅決反對對方的言論，並表明不想再繼續討論時，我們可以說 "Cut it out!" 或是 "Drop it!"，而和此類似的，還有：

> **Give me a break！** （饒了我吧！）
> **Nonsense！**　　　（無稽之談！）

⑤ 直接的反駁，不僅容易製造不融洽的氣氛，也容易造成迴避話題及會話中斷等情況，最好少用。

---

A : Since I work all day, the least you could do is clean the house.

B : *Give me a break*! What do you think I do all day—sit around?

A : I beg to differ! Look at this house!

B : I've had a busy day. Charlie got sick, so I had to take him to the hospital.

A : Oh, I'm sorry. I didn't know that. Look, I didn't mean to argue with you. Let's change the subject!

---

A : 既然我工作了一整天，妳少說也該打掃打掃房子。
B : 饒了我吧！你以為我整天都在做什麼——坐著休息嗎？

A : 我不敢苟同，妳看看這間房子！
B : 我今天很忙。查理生病了，所以我得帶他去醫院。

A : 哦，我很抱歉，我不知道。瞧，我不是故意要和妳吵的，我們換個話題吧！

* ***beg to differ*** (*from sb.*) 不敢苟同；恕難贊同

§ 理想的反駁方法是採取彈性策略(b)，亦即先認可對方所説的，再表明自己的見解。這可説是一種較普遍的反駁方法。此外，以心理學的觀點來看，也是一種有效的方法。其較常出現的説法有以下幾種。

> **Yes, but....**（是的，但～）
>
> **I agree with you but....**（我同意，但是～）
>
> **I see what you mean but....**（我了解你的意思，但～）
>
> **That's more or less true but....**（這沒錯，但～）
>
> **I think that's (partly) true but....**（我想那是眞的，但～）
>
> **I guess you could say that, but I'm afraid....**
> （我想你可以那樣說，但是恐怕～）
>
> **I don't mean to disagree〔͵dɪsəˈgri〕with you, but....**
> （我並不想和你唱反調，但～）
>
> **No offence〔əˈfɛns〕, but....**（不是要冒犯，只是～）
>
> **That's right in theory, but in practice it's impossible.**
> （理論上是對的，但實際上却不可能。）

\* **_more or less_** 或多或少

---

A : Is it still necessary to go over the final details ?

B : **_Yes_**, yes of course, **_but_** I'm afraid we are short of time.

　　A：是不是仍需要再複習最後細節？

　　B：是啊，當然需要，但是恐怕我們的時間不夠。

---

\* **_go over_** 複習　　detail〔ˈditel〕*n.* 細節
**_be short of_** 不足的

A : I have to study for my exam tomorrow.

B : Did you wait until now to prepare for the exam?

A : Yeah, but it's okay. I'll just stay up all night.

B : *I see what you mean, but* you won't be able to perform well if you lack sleep.

A：我必須準備明天的考試。

B：你到現在才開始準備啊？

A：是的，但沒有關係。我要開一整晚的夜車。

B：我了解你的意思，但如果睡眠不足，你是無法考出好成績的。

&ast; *stay up* 熬夜　　perform〔pəˊfɔrm〕*v.* 表現

還有另一種「彈性策略」。在上面的例子中，乃是針對對方所說的話加以肯定，而在另一方面，則可以貶低自己這一方，如以下這一類的話。

**I may be wrong, but....** （也許我錯了，但～）

**I don't know, but....** （我不知道，但是～）

**I'm not sure, but....** （我不確定，但～）

A : I don't think it makes any difference to vote.

B : Every citizen should vote. It's a privilege.

A : *I may be wrong, but* I still can't believe my one vote will make any difference.

A：我認為投票與否沒什麼差別。

B：每位公民都應投票，這是權利。

A：或許我錯了，但我仍不相信我的一票會產生什麼影響。

&ast; vote〔vot〕*v.* 投票　　privilege〔ˊprɪvlɪdʒ〕*n.* 權利

# PRACTICE 6

## PART I

請在空白處填入最適當的「表達個人意見」表現方法。

≪參考答案：p.173≫

(1) A : We can't tell this to Mary. It will break her heart.

B : It's too late. _____, I've already told her the real story.

A : What did she say?

B : She said she understood.


(2) A : Can the children use this playground for practice?

B : Well, _____, non-residents of this town are not permitted（准許）to use the playground, but for a small fee（費用）they can use it for two hours.


(3) A : Current（當前的）articles on criminal rehabilitation（防治）state that the death penalty（刑罰）is no deterrent（遏止）to crime.

B : That isn't true in all cases.

A : What do you mean?

B : _____, such as in the state of Texas, the crime rate dropped after the institution（成立）of the death penalty.

## PART II

請試著將劃線部份語句，改爲較緩和、有彈性的說法。

(1) A : Sara looks better in orange than blue.

B : <u>I disagree. I think she looks good in any color.</u>

A : I don't mean that she looks bad in blue.

B : Well, I think she looks good in blue, too.


(2) A : I think everyone should get married.

B : <u>No, you're wrong! Some people don't want to live with " one person " their entire lives.</u>

A : Well, I think raising a family is the most important thing.


(3) A : The weather report said, " It will rain all weekend."

B : I heard it wouldn't rain on the weekend.

A : <u>I think you're mistaken. The weather report I always listen to is pretty accurate.</u> （準確）

B : When did you hear that report?

A : Earlier this week.

B : Well, I heard the weather report a few minutes ago. I think that report is more accurate.

# 7 You know⋯⋯
## 表現躊躇的心情

與人談話時，碰到不知該如何說，或是因無話可說，而陷入沈思時，往往造成尷尬的沈默。這時便產生了「躊躇」、「修改」的語氣表達法，中文裏有「嗯⋯」，「唉⋯」，「這個嘛⋯」等說詞，在英文中，如下例一般的特殊語氣詞也很常用。

---

A : Yes, Don, what is it?

B : *Um... well...* Shelly, *you, you know...*

A : Yes, Don? I know what?

B : You know how... *uh*... how much... I care about you?

A : What are you getting at?

B : Well, Shelly, I... *uh* I think you're wearing the sweater inside out.

---

A：是，唐，怎麼了？

B：嗯⋯嗯⋯雪莉，妳，妳知道⋯

A：是，唐？我知道什麼？

B：妳知道多⋯啊⋯多麼⋯我多在意妳嗎？

A：你指的是什麼？

B：嗯，雪莉，我⋯啊我想妳把毛衣穿反了。

* *get at* 意指    *inside out* 裏在外地

A : Miss, would you describe the object you saw?

B : *Well*, *uh... well... if...* can you give me a few minutes to gather my thoughts?

A : Sure. But don't take too long. We have to investigate this incident as soon as possible.

B : Well, *I... I... think...* I think... well maybe I didn't see anything.

A : Just take your time and tell me what you saw.

B : Well, it was like this, *uh... I... I... uh...*

---

A : 小姐，妳能描述一下妳所看到的東西嗎？

B : 嗯，啊…嗯…如果…你能給我幾分鐘，整理一下思緒嗎？

A : 當然，但是不要拖太久。我們必須儘快調查這個事件。

B : 嗯，我…我…想…我想…嗯，或許我什麼都沒看到。

A : 妳好好想一下，再告訴我妳所看到的。

B : 嗯，好像是這樣，嗯…我…我…嗯…

\* describe〔dɪˋskraɪb〕*v.* 描述　　gather〔ˋgæðɚ〕*v.* 整理
investigate〔ɪnˋvɛstə,get〕*v.* 調查　*take one's time* 慢慢來

---

A : Hi. Jane! What time do you want to meet for our fishing trip?

B : *Well... uh...* I don't think I can go.

A : When will you know?

B : I don't think I want to go.

A : You mean... you don't want to go?!

B : Yes, that's what I mean.

A：嗨，珍！妳什麼時候要商量釣魚之旅的事？

B：嗯…啊…我想我不能去。

A：妳何時能確定？

B：我不認爲我想去。

A：妳是說…妳不想去？

B：没錯，我就是這個意思。

⑤ 由以上的例子可以知道，「躊躇」及「説話吞吞吐吐」等情況之產生，可能有以下三個原因：⑴説話者驚慌失措，⑵有一些令人感到害羞（embarrassing）的話不得不說，⑶有一些難以啓口的話（如道歉等等）不得不說。在普通的情況下，我們經常可以聽到這些說詞，表現「躊躇」之說法有以下幾種。

| well... （嗯～） | the... er... （這～哦…） |
|---|---|
| uh... （啊～） | a — nd （而～且…） |
| er... （哦～） | I... I... （我～我…） |
| umm... （嗯～） | |

---

A : Thank you for your testimony, Mr. Mayor.

B : My pleasure, your honor. As *I*... have matters to attend to *uh*... at City Hall, *I*... would like to... *uh* leave now.

A : I order you to stay for the entire trial.

B : I don't think you have *the*... *er*... legal right to... *uh* hold me.

A : Believe me, Mr. Mayor, I have the legal authority.

A：謝謝你來作證，市長先生。

B：這是我的榮幸，法官大人。因為我…有事情要處
理啊…在市政府，我…想要…啊現在離開。

A：我命令你待到審判完。

B：我想你…沒有這種權力…阻止我。

A：相信我，市長先生，我有合法的權威。

* testimony〔'tɛstə,monɪ〕*n.* 證言　mayor〔'meɚ〕*n.* 市長
  *your honor* 大人；閣下　attend〔ə'tɛnd〕*v.* 處理
  entire〔ɪn'taɪr〕*adj.* 整個的　trial〔'traɪəl〕*n.* 審判
  legal〔'ligḷ〕*adj.* 合法的　authority〔ə'θɔrətɪ〕*n.* 權威

⑧「躊躇」的功用，是可以對接著要說的話及表現方法做一個選
擇與修飾，也可說是一種拖延時間的策略。對於學習者而言，
選語彙時，考慮文法正確性時，或其他各種想法在腦中閃過時，
就是一種「躊躇」的狀態。除了「嗯」「啊」等語氣詞，表現
「躊躇」的說法還有下列數種。

**(Well) let's see....** （嗯）我們來想想~

**(Well) let me see....** （嗯）讓我想想~

**(Uh) let me think....** （啊）讓我想想~

**You know....** （你知道的~）

**I mean....** （我是說~）

**The thing is....** （事情是這樣的~）

**I can't think of the right expression.** （我想不出適當的措辭。）

**I don't know what to say.** （我不知道說些什麼好。）

**What should I say?** （我該說什麼？）

**The word is at (on) the tip of my tongue**〔tʌŋ〕.
（話已經溜到我嘴邊。）

**I have a mental**〔'mɛntḷ〕**block.** （我腦筋一時轉不過來。）

A： Brian, name two members of the feline family.
B： *Um... let's see... Give me a minute.* Is it a lion... and... and a domestic cat？
A： Yes！ You are right！

  A： 布萊恩，說出兩種貓科動物的名字。
  B： 嗯…讓我想想…給我一分鐘。是獅子…和…和家貓嗎？
  A： 是的！答對了。

\* feline〔'filaɪn〕*adj.* 貓科的
 domestic〔də'mɛstɪk〕*adj.* 居家的

A： The Academy hereby awards you with its highest honor.
B： Thank you. *Uh... I don't know what to say... I can't think of the right expression...* but thank you... thank you very much！ I am just speechless. Thank you all！

  A： 學院在此頒給你最高榮譽。
  B： 謝謝，啊…我不知道說些什麼才好…我想不出適當的表達方式…不過謝謝你們…非常謝謝你們！我說不出話來了。謝謝大家！

\* academy〔ə'kædəmɪ〕*n.* 學院
 hereby〔hɪr'baɪ〕*adv.* 藉此；特此；在此
 award〔ə'wɔrd〕*v.* 頒給
 expression〔ɪk'sprɛʃən〕*n.* 表達
 speechless〔'spitʃlɪs〕*adj.* 說不出話來的

◎ 當自己突然説錯了什麼話時，為免他人誤會，應馬上採取以下的「修正」措施：

**Pardon me**.... （抱歉～）　　**I mean**.... （我是説～）

**Excuse me**.... （對不起～）　**I meant**.... （我是指～）

* pardon〔'pɑrdn̩〕v. 寬恕

---

A：Peter, come here.

B：Who, me?

A：No, I was calling Paul... *I mean* Peter.

---

A：彼得，過來。

B：誰，我嗎？

A：不，我在叫保羅…我是説彼得。

---

A：Driver, please take me to the Met.

B：You mean the Met at the Lincoln Center?

A：Oh, *pardon me*, *I meant* the Museum, not the opera house.

B：Yes, sir.

---

A：司機，請載我到大都會。

B：你是説林肯中心的大都會？

A：哦，抱歉，我是指博物館，不是歌劇院。

B：是，先生。

* Met＝metropolitan〔,mɛtrə'pɑlətn̩〕n. 大都會
*Lincoln Center* 林肯中心　　museum〔mju'ziəm〕n. 博物館
*opera house* 歌劇院

# PRACTICE 7

## PART I

請試著在空白處，使用「躊躇」「欲言又止」的表現方法。

《參考答案：p.173》

(1) A : Sir, I want to return this item (物品).

B : What's wrong with it?

A : The recorder doesn't work on the VCR (錄放影機).

B : ＿＿＿＿＿＿＿＿＿＿＿＿＿＿＿＿＿

A : What's the matter?

B : I'm afraid...uh...that the warranty (保證期限)
has already expired (過期).


(2) A : Tracy, did you forget to do your homework
again ?

B : ＿＿＿＿＿＿＿＿＿＿＿＿＿＿＿

A : Did you, or didn't you?

B : Yes, I did.


(3) A : Would you like to come with Joe and me to see
a play ?

B : ＿＿＿＿＿＿＿＿＿＿＿＿＿＿＿＿

A : Well, maybe some other time.

(4) A : I suppose John will be the next President.

B : Why do you say that?

A : _____

B : Are you just guessing?

A : Yeah, based on the opinion polls（民意調查）.

B : Oh, I see.

## PART II

請在空白處填入表「修正」的表現方法。

(1) A : I wish Dennis would express his true feelings.

B : Have you asked him?

A : No. He's always so offensive（無禮的）.

B : What?

A : _____ "defensive（辯護的）."

B : Maybe you should speak to him truthfully, and he will hopefully answer truthfully.

(2) A : What time will graduation begin?

B : At 1:00 am.

A : At 1:00 am?

B : _____ " pm ", 1:00 pm.

# 8 How about this?

## 改變話題

　　在中文中，我們習慣以「啊」「對了」等來引進新話題，並引起對方的注意，這在前面我們已介紹過了。第一章「喚起對方的注意」中，有"Hey!""Listen!""Look!"等表現方法。在這兒，我們再來看看更典型的「新話題引進」策略。

🔘 首先，我們可用問句「你知道嗎」，一面來引起對方的興趣，
　　一面來當做一種展開新話題的方法。它的說法有以下幾種：

<blockquote>

**You know what ?**（ ↗ ）　（你知道嗎？）
**Guess what.**（ ↘ ）　　（猜猜看。）

</blockquote>

---

A : *Guess what.*（ ↘ ）
B : What ?（ ↘ ）

A : I got a new job !
B : Great ! Where ?

A : At ABC Corporation.

---

A：你猜猜看。
B：什麼？

A：我找到新工作了！
B：太棒了！在哪裏？

A：在ＡＢＣ公司。

* corporation〔͵kɔrpəˈreʃən〕*n.* 公司

若是想要有刺激感，要把令人不敢相信的獨家新聞拿來當做話題，或是想要裝腔作勢地展開談話時，可以採用以下的說法：

**Did I ever tell you that** … ?（我告訴過你～嗎？）

**You'll never guess what happened.**（你一定猜不到發生了什麼事。）

**Listen. I have the most astonishing things to tell you.**
（聽著！我有最驚人的消息要告訴你。）

**You know what Dorothy did?**（你知道桃樂絲做了什麼事嗎？）

**Did you know what happened to Jim?**
（你知道吉姆發生了什麼事嗎？）

* astonishing〔əˈstɑnɪʃɪŋ〕*adj.* 驚人的

A : ***Did I ever tell you that*** Peggy got engaged?
B : What? Are you sure?

A : No, I'm not positive. I'll tell you what. I'll find out for sure.

A：我跟你說過佩姬訂婚了嗎？
B：什麼！？ 你確定？

A：不，我不很肯定。我會告訴你實情，但我得先去證實一下。

* ***get engaged*** 訂婚　　positive〔ˈpɑzətɪv〕*adj.* 肯定的；確信的

A : *You'll never guess what happened.*
B : What?（ ↘ ）

A : Professor Lowe is leaving the university. He has accepted a position in London.
B : When will he leave?

A : He will leave at the end of the semester.

A：你一定猜不到有什麼事發生了？
B：什麼事？

A：羅教授要離開學校了,他已經接受一份在倫敦的工作。
B：他什麼時候走？

A：這學期末他就要離開了。

\* position〔pə'zɪʃən〕 *n.* 職位

🄢 和「話題引進」極為相似的表現方法就是「提議」。在中文裏,我們通常都用「啊！對了,我有一個好主意……」或「這麼做如何呢？」來開頭,將我們的新點子讓別人知道。同樣的,在英文中,也有如下的表現方法。

How about this? 　（這樣好不好？）
I'll tell you what. 　（我會告訴你的。）
Tell you what. 　（告訴你。）

A : I have many errands to do today. I don't think I can take you to the movies.
B : *Tell you what.* Why don't I drive myself to the movies?

A : But I need the car.
B : How about this then? I will ask Paul to drive me.

A：我今天有很多差事要做，我想我大概沒辦法帶妳去去看電影了。

B：告訴你吧！我可以自己開車去看。

A：但是車子我要用。

B：那這樣好不好？我叫保羅開車載我去。

＊ errand〔ˈɛrənd〕 *n.* 差事

◎ 此外，忽然有什麼點子，要將之提出來時，或是要引進什麼新話題時，有以下的說法。

**Hey, I just got an idea.**　（嗨，我剛想到一個點子。）

**I just thought of something.**　（我剛剛想到一件事。）

**What do you think of this idea？**（你覺得這點子如何？）

---

A： *Hey, I just got an idea*！　Let's donate the money to the Children's Zoo.

B：Good idea！But wait... I just thought of something.

A：What？（ ↘ ）

B：The Children's Zoo will be closing next year.

A：Oh, I didn't know that.

B：What do you think of this？We can donate the money to the Hospital Fund.

A：That's a good suggestion.

A：嘿！我剛剛突然想到了！我們把那筆錢捐給兒童動物園。
B：這點子不錯！但是，等等，我剛想到一件事。

A：什麼事？
B：明年兒童動物園就要關閉了。

A：噢，這我不知道。
B：你覺得這樣如何呢？我們可以把錢捐給醫院的基金會。

A：這個提議不錯。

* donate〔do'net〕*v.* 捐贈　　fund〔fʌnd〕*n.* 基金

◎ 為了尋求某些新的點子，在短暫的思考之後，要將自己的想法引入話題時，除了剛才所介紹的"How about this?"及"I'll tell you what."之外，也可以使用以下的表現方法。

**How does this sound?**（這聽起來怎麼樣？）
**I don't know, but one possible idea would be …**
（我不知道，但是比較可行的點子是～）
**I know what we can do.**（我知道我們能做些什麼。）

◎ 和「話題的引進」極為相似的策略是「話題的轉換」。最平常的表現方法就是以「啊，對了…」來開頭，而以下的表現方法也是滿適合的。

**Oh, by the way....**（噢，附帶提一下～）
**Incidentally....**（順便一提～）
**To get off the subject a moment....**（說點題外話～）
**That reminds me of something.**（那讓我想到一件事。）
**I'll tell you what.**（我會告訴你詳情。）
**Do you mind if I change the subject?**
（你介意我換個話題嗎？）
**How about changing the subject?**
（說點別的，如何？）

A : I'm going to Manhattan today.
B : Are you going there for shopping?

A : No. I'm going to the Metropolitan Museum. ***By the way***, can I get a taxi near the museum?
B : It might be difficult, especially on Sunday. You should call a taxi company.

A : That reminds me... I should call my grandmother while I'm in Manhattan.

A：我今天要到曼哈頓去。
B：要去那裏購物嗎？

A：不，我是要去大都會博物館。順便請敎你，在博物館附近有計程車可搭嗎？
B：恐怕很難，尤其是星期天。你應該打電話到計程車公司去。

A：那讓我想到…到曼哈頓時，我該打電話給我祖母。

* Manhattan〔mæn'hætn̩〕*n.* 曼哈頓區
  metropolitan〔,mɛtrə'pɑlətn̩〕*adj.* 大都市的

A : My sister is doing very well in school.
B : Is she in high school now?

A : Yes. She is in her final year. I am very proud of her.
B : ***Incidentally***, have you heard from Marsha?

A : No, why do you ask about her?
B : When you mentioned "high school", I thought of her.

A：我妹妹在學校功課很好。
B：她現在是中學生嗎？

A：是的，在唸高三，我真以她為榮。
B：附帶一提，你收到瑪莎的信了嗎？

A：沒有，你為什麼會問起她？
B：你一提到中學，我就想到她。

\* **hear from** 收到信
mention〔'mɛnʃən〕*v.* 提到

🅢 對於脫離正題的談話，要再回到原主題時，可使用以下的說法：

**To return to our main topic....**
（回到我們的主題～）

**To get back to the point....**（言歸正傳～）

**Let us get back on track....**（我們言歸正傳～）

**Where was I?**（我說到哪了？）

**Anyway....**（無論如何～）

**In any case....**（不管怎樣～）

**All jokes aside....**（說正經的～）

**Seriously though....**（正經地說，儘管～）

**Let's get back to what we were talking about before....**
（在～之前，讓我們回到先前我們所談論的。）

**What were we talking about? Oh, yes. We were talking about....**
（我們剛剛談到什麼？噢，對了，我們是談到～）

\* aside〔ə'saɪd〕*adv.* 在旁地；撇開

A : The Civil War was fought between the Northern and Southern States.

B : Who won?

A : The Northern states won.

B : No, I mean, who won the baseball game last night?

A : Bruce, *let's get back to the subject at hand*!

A：南北戰爭是北方各州與南方各州打仗。

B：誰勝了呢?

A：北方勝了。

B：不是,我是指昨天晚上的棒球比賽,哪一隊獲勝?

A：布魯斯,我們回到手邊的主題上吧!

* *Civil War* 南北戰爭　　northern〔'nɔrðən〕 *adj.* 北方的
southern〔'sʌðən〕 *adj.* 南方的　　state〔stet〕 *n.* 州
*at hand* 手邊的

🔘 相反地,若被要求變更話題,但自己並不希望如此時,有如下的回答方法:

**Please don't change the subject.** (請勿改變話題。)

**Before we begin talking about that, let's finish our discussion at hand.**
(在我們開始討論那件事之前,先結束手邊的話題。)

**Let's not get off the subject.** (我們不要偏離了主題。)

**Would you mind staying with the subject?**
(你介意繼續討論這個主題嗎?)

**I don't want to change the subject.**
(我不想改變話題。)

A : Mrs. Adams, have you been taking your medicine?

B : Where did you study medicine, Doctor?

A : Mrs. Adams, *don't change the subject*. It is
important that you take your medicine!

B : It is also important that I know where you
studied medicine!

A : Harvard University. Now, have you been taking
your medicine?

　　A : 亞當斯太太，妳有持續服藥嗎？
　　B : 你在哪裏唸醫科，醫生？

　　A : 亞當斯太太，不要改變話題。妳是否好好地吃
　　　　藥才重要！
　　B : 知道你在哪裏唸醫科也是一樣重要！

　　A : 哈佛大學。好了，你有持續服藥嗎？

* take〔tek〕*v.* 吃（藥）

被他人要求說明某事或回答某些問題，而自己暫時仍不願去談這
這些事時，也就是希望「延後此一話題」時，有以下的說法。

**I'll get back to you later on that.**
（我等一下再和你談那件事。）

**Could I answer that one later?**
（我可以稍後再回答那個問題嗎？）

Ⓢ 若希望「迴避話題」時，也可以使用如下一般的直接表現方法。

> **Let's not talk about that.** （我們不要談那件事。）
>
> **Let's not bring that up.** （我們不要再提那件事。）
>
> **Let's not go into that.** （不要討論那件事了。）
>
> **I don't feel like talking about that.**
> （我不想談那件事。）
>
> **Let's talk about something else.** （我們談點別的。）
>
> **Oh, perish the thought.** （噢！別那麼想了。）
>
> **Oh, forget it.** （噢，算了吧。）
>
> **Can we change the subject to a more pleasant topic?**
> （我們可不可以換一個比較愉快的話題？）

> \* *bring sth. up* 提起某件事　　*go into* 討論
> perish 〔'perɪʃ〕 *v.* 消失

---

A : Herbert, did you exercise today?
B : *Let's not talk about that.*

A : Why not?
B : It makes me tired talking about exercise.

---

　　A : 赫柏，你今天做過運動了嗎？
　　B : 我們不要談那個。

　　A : 為什麼不？
　　B : 談起運動，我就覺得累。

---

A : Excuse me, sir. May I ask you a few questions?
B : What are they about?

A : The Presidential election.
B : No, *I don't like discussing politics.*

---

A：對不起，先生。我可以問你一些問題嗎？
B：關於哪方面的問題？

A：總統大選。
B：不，我不喜歡談論政治。

* presidential 〔,prɛzə'dɛnʃəl〕 *adj.* 總統的
election 〔ɪ'lɛkʃən〕 *n.* 選舉　　politics 〔'pɑlə,tɪks〕 *n.* 政治

◎ 語氣較強硬的説法有：

**That's none of your business.**
（那不關你的事。）

**Cut it out.** （別説下去了。）

**Drop it.** （別説了。）

◎ 當你完全不想説時，像下列一般，稍微帶著點感情的強硬説法
也有。

**I won't discuss it** ( *with you* ).
〔我不會（和你）談這個。〕

**I don't want to hear your story.**
（我不想聽你説。）

A : Officer, you have the wrong person.
B : You look like the person described in the police report.

A : Let me explain.
B : *I don't want to hear your story.* Let's wait for your lawyer to arrive.

A : But I...
B : Drop it！

　　A : 警官，你捉錯人了。
　　B : 你看起來就像警方報導上描寫的那個人。

　　A : 我可以解釋。
　　B : 我不想聽你說，我們等你的律師來再說吧。

　　A : 但是我…
　　B : 別說了！

＊ describe〔dɪ'skraɪb〕v. 描寫；敍述
　explain〔ɪk'splen〕v. 解釋　　lawyer〔'lɔjɚ〕n. 律師

對於你不太想談的話題，對方却一直說個不停，或是把你的事情拿來開玩笑等等，在這種情況下就可以說：

**Will you get off it？**（別說了好嗎？）

如果對方仍不停止時，就可以說：

**Leave me alone！**（不要煩我！）

# PRACTICE 8

請試著在下列空白處填入適當的會話。〔 提示：(1)～(5)是「 新話
題的引進」，(6)～(7)是「 話題轉換」〕　　《參考答案：p.173 》

(1) A : _____

    B : What ? ( ↘ )

    A : We are getting a new boss. Do you know who
       it is ?

    B : Does it matter who the new boss is ?

    A : No, but I hope things will become better because
       of this change.

(2) A : _____

    B : What ? ( ↘ )

    A : I'm going to college next year.

    B : Oh, yeah ? What will you do there ?

    A : I'm not sure.

    B : Take your time. Don't rush ( 急 ) into a decision.

(3) A : Wow ! Peggy makes a beautiful bride.

    B : Yeah ! She looks like a princess !

    A : _____ Why don't we get
       a picture of her and us together ?

    B : Good idea !

(4) A : I think we should go to Canada for our vacation.

B : _____

A : What ?

B : What do you think of visiting Alaska（阿拉斯加） also?
Alaska is close to Canada.

A : Good idea ! Let's visit Canada and Alaska !


(5) A : _____ We'll have jazz
at the party.

B : I don't like that idea.

A : Why not ?

B : Because it's difficult to dance to jazz.

A : Then, _____ Let's have jazz
during the earlier part of the evening and rock
music later.

B : I don't know. I prefer to have only one type of music.


(6) A : Are you going out ?

B : Yes.

A : Where are you going?

B : To the supermarket.

A : _____ while you're there,
would you buy some orange juice ?


(7) A : Will you attend the World Peace Exhibition（世界和
平展示會） today ?

B : I don't know. I haven't been feeling well. Do you
have any medicine for a headache ?

A : No, I don't._____, I hope to see you there.

# 9 Sorry to interrupt you, but⋯⋯
## 打斷對方的話

🔊 在他人談話的場合中,自己是以第三者的身份,半途插入的情況時,要先引起交談中之雙方的注意,也就是要使用一些「喚起注意」的語氣辭,以下是常見的幾種說法。

**Pardon the interruption, but...** (很抱歉打擾你～)

**I'm sorry** *to interrupt you*, **but...** (很抱歉打擾你～)

**Excuse me** *for interrupting*, **but...** (很抱歉打擾你～)

**May I interrupt you for a moment?**
(我可以麻煩你一下嗎?)

\* interrupt〔ˌɪntəˈrʌpt〕*v.* 打擾

---

A : *I'm sorry to interrupt you, Ms. Wilson, but* if we don't leave now, you'll miss your flight to Moscow.
B : That's right, Mr. Jones. I'll get my suitcase.

---

　　A : 很抱歉,打擾妳了,威爾森小姐。如果我們現在不走的話,妳將會趕不上往莫斯科的飛機了。
　　B : 是的,瓊斯先生,我去拿手提箱。

\* suitcase〔ˈsutˌkes, ˈsjut-〕*n.* 手提箱

A : ***Excuse me for interrupting.*** Would you be interested in purchasing a used car?

B : What kind is it?

A : It's a 1977 Volkswagen Rabbit.

B : No, thanks. I already have a Volkswagen Rabbit.

> A：抱歉，打擾你了。請問你想不想買部二手車？
> B：哪一種車呢？
>
> A：是一九七七年的福斯汽車。
> B：不，謝謝。我已經有一輛了。

* purchase〔'pɜtʃəs,-ɪs〕*v.* 購買
  *a used car* 二手車

自己是站在聽者的立場，當對方說話說到一半時，有所疑問，或是想要有所說明時，上述的方法相當好用。至於其他的表現方法，則有以下幾種。

**Sorry, but I have a question.**（抱歉，我有問題要問。）

**May I ask you a question?**（我可以問你一個問題嗎？）

**I would like to say something.**（我有話要說。）

**Sorry to interrupt you, but...**
（很抱歉打擾你，但是～）

**If I might add a word...**（我想補充一點～）

**Do you mind if I say something?**
（你介不介意我說一些話？）

**Can I say something?**（我能發言嗎？）

A : *Can I say something* ?
B : Sure, go ahead.
A : I don't think you're being fair.
B : Why do you say that ?
A : Because this is the first time you have let me say anything.

A：我能發言嗎？
B：當然，有話直說吧！
A：我覺得你不太公平。
B：爲什麼這麼說呢？
A：因爲這是你第一次允許我發言。

A : Did you hear the announcement ? Ten lucky winners will fly to any city of their choice on Pan Am.
B : *Excuse me for interrupting, Bob, but* I heard "on China Airlines."
A : Right, Lisa. They will also receive $100 in cash.
B : And don't forget a $30,000 car !

A：你聽過那項公告了沒？有十位幸運者可以搭乘泛美航空班機，到他們想去的任何一個城市。
B：對不起，打斷你一下，鮑伯，可是我聽到的是搭中華航空公司的飛機。
A：沒錯，麗莎。他們同時還可得到美金一百元現金。
B：而且別忘了還有一部價值三萬元的車子。

* announcement 〔ə'naʊnsmənt〕 *n.* 通知；公告
pan-〔pæn-〕表「全（all）～」「泛、總（universal）～」之意的綴字形
airlines 〔'ɛr,laɪnz〕 *n. pl.* 航空公司　*in cash* 以現金

Ⓢ 與較親近的同伴談話，想要直接打斷話題，可以說：

**Hold it!** (慢著！)

**Stop it!**（住口！）

**Wait a minute!** (慢著！)

**Wait a sec** (*second* )! (等等！)

---

A : Sue, I can't talk now. I'm late for work.

B : **Hold it, Ken!** Relax. Today is a holiday.

---

A：蘇，我現在沒空跟妳說，我上班要遲到了。

B：慢著，肯恩！別緊張，今天是假日。

* relax〔rɪˈlæks〕 *v*. 放鬆

---

A : Shelly, deliver these packages upstairs and then
finish this pile of work. Then go....

B : **Wait a minute, Susan!** Who's in charge here, you
or Mr. Foley?

---

A：雪莉，把這些包裹送到樓上去，然後把這堆工作
做完。然後去…

B：慢著，蘇珊！誰是這裏的主管，妳，還是傅雷先
生？

* deliver〔dɪˈlɪvə〕 *v*. 遞送
upstairs〔ˈʌpˈstɛrz〕 *adv*. 向樓上
pile〔paɪl〕 *n*. 一堆

◎ 對方所說的，有不對的地方時，可以使用如下一般的打斷方法：

> A : Hurry, Tommy! You're going to be late for school!
> B : *But Mom*....
>
> A : The bus is coming....
> B : But Mom....
>
> A : Hurry....
> B : But Mom, today is Sunday!

A：快點，湯米！你上學要遲到了！
B：但是，媽…

A：公車就快來了…
B：但是，媽…

A：快呀！
B：可是，媽媽，今天是星期天！

◎ 當「打斷」被允許時，則對方可能會回答：

Yes?（ ↗ ）　　（怎麼？）
Sure, go ahead.　（請說下去！）

◎ 但是，當他（她）不希望被打斷時，則會說：

Hold on a minute.（等一下。）
Could you hold on a minute?（你等一下，好嗎？）
OK, but let me just finish.（好的，不過讓我說完一下。）
May I finish?（可以聽我說完嗎？）
I want to say one more thing.（我還有一件事要說。）
Please don't interrupt. Hear me out, please.
（請不要插嘴，請聽我把話說完。）

\* *hear sb. out* 聽某人把話說完

☺ 要打消打岔念頭，並聽對方說完，可以讓步的口吻說：

**Of course, go ahead.**　（當然，說下去。）
**Sorry. Go ahead.**　（很抱歉，請繼續說。）
**Yes. Sorry.**　（是的，對不起。）
**Sure, I will.**　（當然，我會的。）

A : Last Sunday I went to a nice French restaurant...
B : Excuse me for interrupting, but which one?

A : The one on Broadway and 57th Street. And I was
waiting for my date to arrive....
B : *Sorry*, but who was your date?

A : My girlfriend, Amy....
B : *Sorry again*, what's her last name?

　　A : 上禮拜天我去了一家很棒的法國餐廳…
　　B : 對不起，打斷你一下，是哪一家呢？

　　A : 在百老滙五十七街的那一家。當時我正在等我女
　　　　朋友來…。
　　B : 對不起，你約了誰呢？

　　A : 我的女朋友，艾美…
　　B : 對不起，她姓什麼？

* Broadway 〔'brɔd,we〕 *n.* 百老滙（New York 市南北向的一條
大街，為戲院、夜總會等的集中地）
date 〔det〕 *n.* 約會的對方（異性）

# PRACTICE 9

請試著運用「打斷話題」的表現方法，完成下列對話。〔(1)、(2)
中，假設 A 正和同伴說話，而 B 以第三者的身份來打斷 A 說話〕

《 參考答案：p.174 》

(1) （B 為第三者）

A： I can't wait to see the show. Last year....

B： _____

A： _____


(2) （B 為第三者）

A： I'm from New York and....

B： _____

A： _____


(3) A： After dating for six years, Bruce and Tammy got
married....

B： _____

A： _____


(4) A： I'm so happy that I came to this university. The
academic (學術的) standards are the best in the United
States.

B： _____

A： _____

(5) A : The southeast portion of Louisiana is being hit by
     Hurricane (颱風) Florence and....

　　B : _____

　　A : _____


(6) A : Doris is going to the states and....

　　B : _____

　　A : _____

# 10 *That's great!*
## 積極回應對方的話

在與他人對話時，聽的人應該讓對方知道自己正在聽著。也就是說，聽的人有所反應時，在必要時，可以藉著語言的或非語言的方法，如點頭（nodding），來讓對方知道。語言上的方法有下面幾種。

(a)重覆。　(b)隨聲附和。　(c)驚訝、同感的表現。

(d)憤怒、同情的表現。　(e)其他。

☺「重覆」是一種效果非常好的英文學習法，亦即對於自己有興趣的部分，再向對方探詢一遍，來當作一種訊號，使會話能順暢地進行下去。下面的三組對話是典型的例子。

---

A : Bob and Jane are going to break up.

B : *Bob and Jane are going to break up*? ( ↗ )

A : Yeah. Can you believe it ?

---

　　　A：鮑伯和珍要分手了。

　　　B：鮑伯和珍要分手？

　　　A：沒錯，你相信嗎？

\* *break up* 分手

A : I told him to break up with her.
B : *You told him to break up with her*?

　　A：我叫他和她分手。
　　B：你叫他和她分手？

A : Is there anything else you want me to do ?
B : *Is there anything else I want you to do*? Hmmm...
No. Nothing I can think of at this moment.

　　A：你還有別的事要我做嗎？
　　B：我還有別的事要你做嗎？嗯⋯没有，現在我還没
　　　　想到什麼事。

∽ 在中文的對話中，為了表示自己有在傾聽，都會不經意地附和
一下，如「啊！是啊。」「真的？」「嗯！」「對啊！」等等字
眼。在英文中亦然，下列是幾個較常用的說法。

Uh-huh. （↗）　　（嗯。）　　Really? （↗）（真的？）
Is that right ?（↗）（真是那樣嗎？）　Oh, yeah?（↗）(哦,是嗎？)
I know what you mean.（我懂你的意思。）　I see. （我明白。）
Sure. （當然。）　　　　　　　　Of course. （當然。）

A : The temperature is supposed to be 15° below
zero tomorrow.
B : *Really? Is that right* ?

A : Well, that's what the newspaper said.
B : Uh-huh....

A : So, if you go outside without your winter-coat,
you'll catch a cold.
B : That's for sure.

A：明天氣溫可能會降到零下十五度。
B：眞的？眞是那樣嗎？

A：嗯，那是報上說的。
B：嗯……

A：所以，如果你不穿大衣就到外面的話，會感冒。
B：那是當然的。

* temperature〔'tɛmprətʃɚ〕*n.* 溫度
  winter-coat〔'wɪntɚ,kot〕*n.* 大衣

◎ 對方在說某些有趣的或是可怕的事時，可以表現出驚訝、同感
或感激的語氣，使對話氣氛熱絡。此外，配合談話的內容，也
可以加入各種具有 positive 意味的形容詞（如：smart, nice,
terrific, ingenious 等等），自己勇敢地去嘗試各種說法，將
會有意想不到的效果喔！

**Wow!** （哇！）　**That's great!** （太棒了！）
**Fantastic!** （太妙了！）　**That's wonderful!** （好極了！）
**How nice!** （太好了！）　**Beautiful!** （美極了！）
**Oh, I love it!** （噢，我愛死了！）　**What a great idea!** （多棒的主意！）
**I'm so glad to hear that!** （我好高興聽到這樣！）

* fantastic〔fæn'tæstɪk〕*adj.* 太妙了

---

A : Did you see the football game yesterday?
B : No. What happened?

A : In the final seconds of the game, the Giants'
    quarterback threw a touchdown pass.
B : *Wow! That's great!* I bet all the fans went
    crazy!

A：你昨天看了足球賽沒有？

B：沒有，怎麼了？

A：比賽結束前幾秒，巨人隊的四分後衛使了一記觸地得分。

B：哇！太棒了！我打賭所有球迷都爲之瘋狂。

\* quarterback〔'kwɔrtɚ,bæk〕*n.* 四分後衛　throw〔θro〕*v.* 投；丟
touchdown〔'tʌtʃ,daʊn〕*n.* 觸地得分　fan〔fæn〕*n.* 球迷

⑤ 下列的「天啊！」「真的？」等說法，若能以一種頑皮嬉戲的
表情及聲音來説的話，效果更佳。

**You're kidding**〔'kɪdɪŋ〕.　　　　**No kidding!**

**Oh, my God!**　　　　　　　　**Oh my gosh**〔gɑʃ〕**!**

**Good heavens!**　　　　　　　**Really?**（ ↗ ）

**Are you sure?**（ ↗ ）　　　　**Holy**〔'holɪ〕**cow!**

A : Harry is leaving for London tomorrow.
B : *You're kidding*! That's great!

A : He's going to stay there for a month.
B : Oh my gosh! Is it a business trip?

A : No. He's going to tour the major museums.
B : Wow! That sounds interesting!

A：哈利明天要去倫敦。

B：你在開玩笑吧！那真是太好了！

A：他要在那兒待一個月。

B：哦，天啊！這趟是商務之旅嗎？

A：不，他要去參觀各大博物館。

B：哇！聽起來似乎很有趣！

\* tour〔tʊr〕*v.* 參觀　major〔'medʒɚ〕*adj.* 較大的；主要的

🔊 聽到一些令人垂頭喪氣的事時，就可以使用一些失望、灰心、
憤怒的表現方法，如「我的天啊！」「可惡！」等。特別的是，在
美國社會中，像這一類的 swear-words 很多。

| | |
|---|---|
| **What a drag!**（眞討厭！／多累贅啊！） | **What a pain!**（多痛苦啊！） |
| **What a nuisance!**（多討厭啊！） | **That stinks!**（好臭啊！） |
| **That's disgusting!**（好噁心啊！） | **Oh, no!**（哦，不！） |
| **Oh my gosh!**（哦，糟了！） | **My goodness!**（我的天啊！） |
| **Gee!**（啊！） | **Shoot!**（可惡！） |
| **Oh, brother!**（哦，老兄！） | **Oh, nuts!**（哦，瘋子！） |
| **Rats!**（胡扯！） | **Oh, dear.**（哎呀，天哪！） |

* drag〔dræg〕*n.* 拖累的東西；累贅
  nuisance〔'njusn̩s〕*n.* 討厭的人或事物
  stink〔stɪŋk〕*v.* 發臭　　disgusting〔dɪs'ɡʌstɪŋ〕*adj.* 噁心的
  gee〔dʒi〕*interj.* 表示驚奇強調等的感嘆語
  shoot!〔ʃut〕*interj.* 可惡（代替 *shit*）
  nuts〔nʌts〕*n.* 瘋子　　rats〔ræts〕*n.* 鼠；胡說八道

---

A : Richie, I have bad news for you.
B : *Oh, no* ! What is it?

A : Your father came to get you.
B : What a drag ! Oh, I don't want to go home....

---

A：理奇，我要告訴你個壞消息？
B：哦，不！是什麼壞消息？

A：你父親來接你。
B：眞討厭！哦，我不想回家…。

🕲 表示「受夠了」的樣子時，則有以下幾種表示方法。

| | |
|---|---|
| **C'mon.** ( *Come  on* ) | （得了吧！） |
| **Don't  tell  me.** | （別開玩笑了！） |
| **You're  kidding.** | （你在開玩笑吧！） |
| **You're  nuts**〔nʌts〕**.** | （你瘋了！） |
| **You('re)  crazy.** | （你瘋了！） |
| **You're  too  much.** | （你眞令人受不了！） |
| **Give  me  a  break.** | （饒了我吧！） |
| **Don't  get  carried  away.** | （少神經了！） |

---

A : Rainy days make me feel sad.
B :  I always sing in the rain.

A : You're weird !
B : *C'mon* !  That's not very nice.

---

　　A：雨天使我感到悲傷。
　　B：我總是在雨中唱歌。

　　A：你眞奇怪！
　　B：拜託！你這樣講不對哦！
　　　（別這樣講嘛！）

＊ weird〔wɪrd〕*adj*. 奇怪的

◎ 同情對方時，應如何表示比較好呢？表示同情時，乃是由於對方遭遇到困難或是悲傷的事情，因此，我們應給他（她）一些懇摯的安慰如下。當然，最重要的是要放入感情。

**That's too bad.** （眞是太糟了。）

**What a pity！** （多可惜啊！）

**Better luck next time.** （下次運氣會好些。）

**I'm sorry to hear that.** （聽到這件事我很難過。）

**It must be pretty rough**〔rʌf〕**on you.** （你一定很不好過。）

**I know how you must feel.** （我知道你的感受。）

**I understand.** （我了解。）

**What a shame**〔ʃem〕**.** （多可惜啊！）

---

A : I flunked my math exam.

B : *Tough luck*！

---

A：我數學當掉了。

B：你眞倒楣！

* flunk〔flʌŋk〕*v.* 當掉

tough〔tʌf〕*adj.* 艱難的；不順利的

◎ 我們也可以鼓勵對方。配合著當時的情況，可以分別使用以下的表現方法。

**Cheer up.** （振作點！高興點！）

**Keep it up.** （繼續努力！）

**Don't give up.** （別放棄！）

**Hang**〔hæŋ〕**in there.** （堅持下去！）

**Stick with it.** （堅持下去！）

**Don't worry. You can make it.** （別擔心，你可以做到的。）

**Everything is going to be all right.** （所有事情都會逐漸好轉的。）

§ 其他的表現方法中，則有一些表示不太關心的説法。

> **So what？** （那又怎樣？）
>
> **Who cares？** （誰在乎？）
>
> **What difference does it make？** （這樣有何差別？）
>
> **It's all the same to me.** （對我來說，都是一樣的。）
>
> **What can I do？** （我能做什麼？）
>
> **Oh, yeah？** （哦，是嗎？）

> ☞ "Oh, yeah？"可因語調不同，產生多種效果，可表「附和」、「驚訝」或「不在乎」的語氣。

§ 使用下列幾種説法，可表現出有興趣聽別人説下去的語氣。

> **And？（ ♪ ）** （然後呢？）
>
> **And then what happened？** （然後發生什麼事？）
>
> **Then what？** （然後怎樣？）

§ 以上是一些表示「回應」的方法，接下來是説話者這一方面。當我們不知道對方是否有在聽時，應該如何確定呢？

> **What's the matter？** （怎麼了？）
>
> **What's wrong？** （有什麼不對勁嗎？）
>
> **Are you OK？** （你還好吧？）
>
> **Is anything wrong？** （有什麼不對嗎？）
>
> **What are you thinking about？** （你在想什麼？）
>
> **What's on your mind？** （你在想什麼？）
>
> **Is something bothering you？** （有什麼事困擾你嗎？）
>
> **What's bugging you？** （你在煩些什麼？）
>
> **Are you with me？** （你有在聽嗎？）
>
> **Are you listening to me？** （你有在聽我説話嗎？）

> \* bug〔bʌg〕 *v.* 使煩惱

🔊 對於對方所說的話，想要加以「補充」，可以有下列幾種說法。

**That brings up another point....**
（那就引出另一個重點～）

**Relating what you have said,....**
（重述你所說過的～）

**Let me piggyback on what you have just said....**
（讓我引述你剛才說的～）

**If I might add a word....**
（容我再說一句話～）

**Let me add something** (*to what you have said*)....
〔讓我補充幾點（有關你所說的）～〕

**May I add something to what has been said?**
（我能補充幾點嗎？）

**I would like to comment on that.**
（我願意對那件事提出說明。）

**In addition to what you have just said,....**
（除了你剛說的之外，～）

**Concerning the point you have just brought up,....**
（關於你剛提出的那點～）

**I would like to say something about what you have just said.**
（對於你剛說的，我想要補充幾句。）

* ***bring up*** 引出　　relate〔rɪˈlet〕*v*. 重述；關於
　piggyback〔ˈpɪgɪˌbæk〕*v*. 引述；揹著
　comment〔ˈkɑmɛnt〕*v*. 提出說明

A : The youth of today are the leaders of tomorrow.
B : And, our future depends greatly on them!

A : Furthermore, they need proper role models !
B : *If I may add a word again*, it's important for us to inspire them !

　　A：今日的青年是明日的主人翁！
　　B：那，我們的未來十分仰仗他們囉！

　　A：再者，他們需要正確的行為楷模！
　　B：容我再說一句，我們去啓發他們才重要！

* leader〔'lidə〕 *n.* 主人翁；領導者　　*depend on* 仰賴
proper〔'prɑpə〕 *adj.* 正確的　 role〔rol〕 *n.* 角色
model〔'mɑdḷ〕 *n.* 楷模　inspire〔ɪn'spaɪr〕 *v.* 啓發

A : Crime, poverty and education are the major issues of this Presidential campaign.
B : And yet none of the candidates are discussing these issues.

A : *That brings up another point*. Why is the press focusing on issues other than these ?

　　A：犯罪、貧窮和教育是這次總統大選的主要論點。
　　B：然而還沒有一個候選人談到這幾點。

　　A：這就引出另一個問題。為什麼新聞界強調這些以外的問題？

* crime〔kraɪm〕 *n.* 犯罪　　 poverty〔'pɑvətɪ〕 *n.* 貧窮
issue〔'ɪʃʊ,'ɪʃjʊ〕 *n.* 問題；爭論點
condidate〔'kændə,det,'kændədɪt〕 *n.* 候選人
*the press* 新聞界　　 *focus on* 強調

◎ 對於自己所説的，要加以補充時，應如何做呢？

**Besides,....**（除此之外，～）　　**On top of that,....**（除此之外,～）

**Furthermore,....**（再者～）　　**In addition,....**（此外，～）

**Moreover,....**（此外，～）　　**Not that alone,....**（不只那樣,～）

---

A : Our tenants association has a list of demands to
　　give to the landlord.

B : If we don't receive our demands, we will take legal
　　action. ***On top of that***, we'll have a rent strike !

---

　　A : 我們租屋者聯盟將對房東提出一些要求。

　　B : 如果要求無法得到回應，我們將採取法律途徑。
　　　　除此之外，我們還將發動罷租行動！

\* tenant〔'tɛnənt〕*n.* 租屋者；房客
　 association〔ə,sosɪ'eʃən,ə,soʃɪ'eʃən〕*n.* 聯盟
　 demand〔dɪ'mænd〕*n.* 要求　　landlord〔'lænd,lɔrd〕*n.* 房東
　 rent〔rɛnt〕*n.* 承租　　strike〔straɪk〕*n.* 罷工

---

A : I'd like to complain about the repairs you did to
　　my car.

B : Yes, sir, what is it?

A : The brakes still don't seem to be working
　　properly and ***on top of that***, there's something
　　wrong with the gear box !

---

　　A：上次你替我修的車，我要申訴。

　　B：哦，先生，怎麼了？

　　A：煞車似乎仍不太靈光，除此之外，變速機箱也有
　　　　問題！

\* complain〔kəm'plen〕*v.* 訴苦　　brakes〔breks〕*n.pl.* 剎車

🎧 相當於「…等等」的英文表現，有以下幾種。

**and so on**

**and so forth**

**and things like that**

**and God knows what else**

**et cetera** [ɛtˈsɛtrə]

**or whatever**

**the list goes on and on**

🎧 我們最後來舉一個例子，看看其使用方法。

---

... VOA broadcasts primarily news that takes up about one half of our format. The rest of the time you can hear rock'n'roll music and old standards like Frank Sinatra. There's "Press Conference U.S.A." and "American Viewpoints". There are weekly surveys of world news, correspondent's reports, music, cultural events, features, *the list goes on and on.*

---

VOA 電台主要播報新聞，這些新聞佔了我們節目形式的一半。其餘的時間你可以聽到搖滾樂，和像法蘭克辛那屈演唱的典型老歌。然後還有"美國記者會"、"美國瞭望"以及一週世界新聞概觀、通訊記者報導、音樂、文化活動、特寫等等。

* broadcast [ˈbrɔd͵kæst] v. 廣播    **take up** 佔據
  format [ˈfɔrmæt] n. 形式    **rock'n'roll** 搖滾
  standard [ˈstændəd] n. 標準；典型
  **press conference** 記者會    viewpoint [ˈvju͵pɔɪnt] n. 觀點
  survey [ˈsɝve, səˈve] n. 概觀    feature [ˈfitʃə] n. 特寫
  correspondent [͵kɔrəˈspɑndənt] n. 通訊記者

# PRACTICE 10

## PART I

請依括弧中提示的「反應」，試著填入不同的說法。

《參考答案：p.174》

(1) There was a plane crash（失事）in Germany！

    (a)（重覆）　_____

    (b)（附和）　_____

    (c)（驚訝）　_____

    (d)（同情）　_____


(2) The ski（滑雪）trip is canceled！

    (a)（重覆）　_____

    (b)（氣餒）　_____

    (c)（憤怒）　_____

    (d)（其他）　_____


(3) Bob and Jane are getting married！

    (a)（重覆）　_____

    (b)（驚訝）　_____

    (c)（高興）　_____

    (d)（其他）　_____

(4) John is going to be the next President of the United States !

    (a) （重覆）＿＿＿＿＿＿＿＿＿＿＿＿

    (b) （附和）＿＿＿＿＿＿＿＿＿＿＿＿

    (c) （不關心）＿＿＿＿＿＿＿＿＿＿

    (d) （補充）＿＿＿＿＿＿＿＿＿＿＿

## PART II

請在空白的部分，填入「補充」的表現方法。

(1) A : I think Bob is very handsome.

    B : Does he find you attractive（有魅力的）also？

    A : I don't know, but he's certainly attractive to me.

    B : ＿＿＿＿＿＿＿＿＿＿＿＿, you are crazy about him.

(2) A : I want to call my parents, but long distance calls are too expensive.

    B : Why don't you write to them？

    A : That's a good idea! They'll appreciate my letters!

    B : ＿＿＿＿＿＿＿＿, you can save money!

# 11 | *Let's get together sometime.*
劃下完美的休止符

　　會話好比唱歌，總有結束的時候，如何完美地劃下休止符，並給雙方留下愉快的印象，跟開始談話時要引起對方注意一樣重要。本章便要剖析結束談話前，您該怎麼說來表示與某人談得很愉快，或因某些原因得道再見，或對方這麼說時，您該怎樣回答才好等等。

🜚 與對方高興地談完一段話後，應該說句類似「幸會！」的話，常　用的說法有下列幾種。

> **It's been nice talking with you.** （和你談話真愉快。）
>
> **I've really enjoyed talking to you.** （我真的很喜歡和你說話。）
>
> **Great seeing you.** （看到你真好。）
>
> **I hope we get a chance to get together soon.**
> （我希望我們很快就有機會聚在一起。）
>
> **I'm looking forward to meeting you again.**
> （我期望再見到你。）
>
> **It was good seeing you.** （見到你真好。）
>
> **Good seeing you.** （高興見到你。）
>
> **Nice meeting you.** （高興碰到你。）

A : Well, *it was good seeing you.*

B : Good seeing you, too.

A : Goodbye.

B : Take care.

---

A : 嗯，見到你眞好！

B : 我也很高興見到你！

A : 再見。

B : 保重。

\* *take care* 保重

☞ 這兒，令我們想到一開始見面的寒喧話 "Good to see you."。這句話之所以使用不定詞 to，乃是表示現在即將發生，以及將繼續發生的事；使用 ing 的情況，乃是表示現在正在進行，或是即將結束。因此（當然也會有一些例外），

→ 見面的時候：Nice to see you.

→ 告別的時候：Nice seeing you.

此外，順便一提，同樣是「見面」，但是和好朋友見面時，要用 see，而和未知的陌生人初次相遇時，則用 meet。

Ⓢ 想結束會話時，則應舉一些如下的理由（ excuse ── 可能是真的，也可能是假的 ），再離開現場會比較好。

I'd like to talk to you more about this, but I'd better be getting back to work.

（我想要跟你多談談這個，但是我得回去工作了。）

Nice talking with you, but I'd better get going. My boss must be waiting for me.

（很高興和你談天，但我得走了，我老闆一定在等我了。）

I'm sorry I can't talk any more, but I have an appointment at six. （很抱歉我不能再聊了，我六點跟人有約。）

A : *Well, I have to go now. I must finish my work.*
B : Okay, call me later to confirm our weekend plans.

A : Alright, talk to you later.

　　A：嗯，我得走了，我必須做完我的工作。
　　B：好，晚點打電話給我，以商榷我們的週末計劃。

　　A：好的，晚點再跟你聊。
　　＊ confirm〔kən'fɝm〕*v.* 商榷　alright〔ɔl'raɪt〕*adv.* 好的

◎ 若要顧及「尊重」對方的立場來結束會話的話，則有以下的說法。

**I'm sorry to have taken up so much of your time.**
（我很抱歉耽誤你那麼多時間。）

**Sorry to have bothered you.** （真抱歉打擾你了。）
**Well, I'll stop bothering you now.** （嗯，我不打擾你了。）
**I'll let you go** *(back to work)*. 〔我會放你走（回去工作）。〕
**I'll let you go now.** （我現在讓你走。）
**I don't want to keep you from your work any more.**
（我不想再耽誤你的工作了。）
**I'm sorry I kept you so long.** （我很抱歉耽誤你這麼久。）

A : *Sorry I kept you too long.*
B : That's all right. I'm glad you called. So long.

A : So long.

　　A：抱歉耽誤你太久。
　　B：沒關係，我很高興你打電話來，再見！

　　A：再見！

　　＊ *so long* 再見

A : *... other than that, I don't have any other news.*
B : All right. Thanks for the information.
A : You are very welcome.

> A :…除此之外，我沒有其它消息。
>
> B :好的，謝謝你通知我。
>
> A :不客氣。

若對方也認為談話應該結束了時，對於「非常愉快」的表現方法（如 " It's been a pleasure talking with you. "），我們有以下幾種比較適當的回答。

**Yes, I've enjoyed it, too.** （是的，我也很喜歡和你談話。）
**It was good to see you.** （見到你真好。）
**Maybe we can talk again.** （也許我們能再談談。）
**Let's get together again sometime.** （有時間我們再聚聚。）
**It was fun.** （真有趣。）
**Same here.** （我也一樣。）

A : It's been a pleasure seeing you.
B : *Maybe we can get together some other time....*
A : Yeah. And thanks again. See you later.
B : Oh, see you later.

> A :看到你真愉快。
>
> B :也許改天我們可以再聚聚…。
>
> A :是啊！再次謝謝你，再見。
>
> B :哦，再見。

✆ 雙方結束會話，要分開的時候，不要忘記以下的表現方法。

**Bye-now.** （拜拜。）

**So long.** （再見。）

**Take it easy.** （放輕鬆點。） **Take care.** （保重。）

**Have a nice day** (*weekend, evening, etc.*)!
〔玩得愉快！祝你有愉快的一天（周末、夜晚等）！〕

(*I'll*) **see you later.** （待會見。）

(*I'll*) **see you around.** （待會見。）

(*I'll*) **talk to you later.** （待會再和你說。）

**Good luck with your exam.** （祝你考試順利。）

**Good night, John.** （晚安，約翰。）

**I'll be in touch.** （我會保持聯繫。）

**I'll be thinking of you.** （我會想念你的。）

**I'll call you soon.** （我會儘快打電話給你。）

---

A : Who is it?

B : Mailman! I have a package for Susan Jackson.

A : I am Susan Jackson.

B : Please sign this release form.

A : Thank you!

B : *Have a nice day*!

---

A：誰？

B：郵差，我這兒有個包裹要給蘇珊・傑克森。

A：我就是蘇珊・傑克森。

B：請簽這張收據。

A：謝謝！

B：祝妳有愉快的一天。

# PR**A**CTICE 11

請利用以下的每一個句子，各自完成一段「終止會話」的對話。

《參考答案：p.175》

(1) It's been great seeing you again.

(2) My phone bill （費用） is going to be very high, I'd better hang up （掛電話）

(3) I'm sorry to have taken up so much of your time. I'd better let you go.

(4) Let's get together sometime.

# II

## PART

精通口語英會第12招－
自我表現句型40

Expressing Yourself in English

▲▲▲▲▲ ━━━描述「我」的慣用句型

# 1 我是～
# *I am*～

■ 説明身分・職業 ━━━━━━━

- a student. （我是學生。）
- 〔klɜk〕*n*. ● a bank ***clerk***. （我是銀行職員。）
- an office worker. （我是上班族。）
- a secretary. （我是秘書。）
- 〔'selzmən〕*n*. ● a ***salesman***. （我是推銷員。）
- a salesperson. （我是售貨員。）
- a computer specialist. （我是電腦專家。）
- 〔ə'kaʊntənt〕*n*. ● an ***accountant***. （我是會計。）

■ 説明自己的狀態 ━━━━━━

- hungry. （我肚子餓。）
- very angry. （我很生氣。）
- very sad. （我很難過。）
- very happy. （我很快樂。）
- thirsty. （我口渴。）
- nearsighted. （我有近視。）
- 〔'nɜvəs〕*adj*. ● ***nervous***. （我很緊張。）
- in trouble. （我有困難。）
- broke now. （我現在沒錢。）
- not good with machines. （我對機械專業知識懂得很少。）
- poor with mechanical things. （我不懂機械方面的知識。）

■ 説明自己的感受 ─────

- interested in movies. (我對電影有興趣。)
- tired of that story.
  ( 那段故事我聽厭了。)
- bored. ( 我很無聊。)

■ 説明所在及年齡 ─────

- here. ( 我在這裡。)
- in New York. ( 我在紐約。)
- in my twenties. ( 我二十幾歲。)
- in my late twenties. ( 我將近三十歲了。)
- from Taipei. ( 我來自台北。)

☆ 用 **I am**⋯開頭的時候，通常有 **A＝B** 的關係，因此，*I am a Chinese.*
（我是中國人。）句中，" a Chinese " 就是 " I "，符合了 A＝B 的公式。
而 *I am very hungry.* （我很餓。）的情形也是一樣，" very hungry " 的
人指的就是 " I "。但是 A＝B 的公式也有不成立的時候，如 *I am going
outside.* （我要出門了。）句中的現在進行式用法，就不屬於 A＝B 的
關係。I am 在會話時常縮寫為 I'm，請利用例句將 I am 用 Are you 的
第二人稱疑問詞代換為問句。

我有～
*I have～*

■ 表示自己所有 ─────

- a personal computer. (我有一台個人電腦。)

■ 表示自己飼養 ─────

- a nice cat. ( 我養了一隻可愛的貓 。)

■ 說明自己的人際關係 ————————————

- a family. （我有一個家。）

- two brothers and one sister.
  （我有兩個兄弟和一個妹妹。）

- a friend in the United States.
  （我有一個朋友住在美國。）

■ 有某種消息的說法 ————————————

- a good idea. （我有一個好主意。）

- good news for you.（我有好消息要告訴你。）

■ 說明食慾狀態 ————————————

〔ˈæpəˌtaɪt〕 *n.* • no ***appetite*** at all.（我一點食慾也沒有。）

- had enough.（我吃飽了。）

■ 說明自己有預定計劃 ————————————

- an appointment. （我有個約會。）

- a meeting this afternoon.
  （今天下午我要參加一個會議。）

- work this weekend. （這個週末我要工作。）

■ 說明責任、興趣 ————————————

〔rɪˌspɑnsəˈbɪlətɪ〕 *n.* • ***responsibility*** for this work.
（我負責這件工作。）

〔kin〕 *adj.* • a ***keen*** interest in you.（我對你很有興趣。）

☆ 用 **I have** 開頭的句子，其後必定有「物」（受詞）。*I have no appetite.*
（我沒有食慾。）句中，" appetite " 就是所謂的「物」。*I had enough.* 或
是*I' ve had enough.*（我吃飽了。）是在吃飯時的說法，其中的受詞即被
省略。另外也有 I have to ….（我必須～）的說法，例如*I have to finish
this work first.*（我必須先完成這項工作。）I had enough. 是 I had
enough of it.的省略形，但不可說成 I had it enough.

# 3

我在~工作。
## I work for~

- a bank. （我在銀行做事。）

[ˈgʌvənmənt] *n.*
- the ***government***. （我在公家機關做事。）

- a hospital. （我在醫院工作。）

[ˈdilə] *n.*
- a computer ***dealer***. （我在電腦銷售公司做事。）

[moˈtel] *n.*
- a ***motel***. （我在汽車旅館做事。）

- an English conversation school.
  （我在英語會話學校做事。）

- a trading company. （我在貿易公司做事。）

- a publishing company. （我在出版社做事。）

[ˈtrævl̩ ˈedʒənsɪ]
- a ***travel agency***. （我在旅行社做事。）

[ˈrɪəl əˈstet]
- a ***real estate*** agency. （我在房地產公司做事。）

[stɑk] *n.*
- a ***stock*** company. （我在證券公司做事。）

☆ **I work for....** 是被問及***what do you do***？（你從事哪種工作？）時的回答方法。
I work for a bank. 和 *I'm a bank clerk*. （我是銀行職員。）意思相同。如果
是自己營業時，可回答 *I'm self-employed*. （我自己經營。）當被問到*what kind
of work do you do*？（你做哪種工作？）時，也可具體地回答: *I sell jeans,
shirts, and jackets*. （我賣牛仔褲、襯衫和夾克。）

# 4

描述自己意見的慣用句型

我會~ / 我將~
## I'll~

■ 說明最近將做之事 ————————

- call you. （我會打電話給你。）

　　　　　　　　● pick you up right away. ( 我立刻來接你。)

〔faɪl〕*n.* ● find that *file*. ( 我會找到那個檔案。)

■ 描述自己的意願 ─────────

　　　　　　　　● have steak. ( 我要一客牛排。)

　　　　　　　　● support you. ( 我會支持你。)

　　　　　　　　● do it. ( 我會做。)

　　　　　　　　● think about it. (我會考慮一下。)

　　　　　　　　● answer the phone. ( 我來接電話。)

　　　　　　　　● answer the door. ( 我去開門。)

　　　　　　　　● pay for the movie. ( 我來付電影票錢。)

☆ **Will** 可表示意志或是未來將做之事，例如 *I' ll call you.* 是指「我待會兒打電話給你。」，而 *I' ll support you.* ( 我會支持你。) 則是表達意志或決心的說法。I' ll 是 I will 的縮寫。

# 5

▲ ▲ ▲ ▲ 描述自己喜好的慣用句型

我喜歡～
## I like～

　　　　　　　　● you. ( 我喜歡你。)

　　　　　　　　● him. ( 我喜歡他。)

　　　　　　　　● this book. ( 我喜歡這本書。)

　　　　　　　　● that movie. ( 我喜歡那部電影。)

　　　　　　　　● that color. (我喜歡那個顏色。)

〔'sɛns əv'hjumɚ〕 ● your *sense of humor*.
　　　　　　　　　　( 我喜歡你的幽默感。)

〔'ætməs,fɪr〕*n.* ● this *atmosphere*. ( 我喜歡這種氣氛。)

 • this music. ( 我喜歡這種音樂。)

  • your figure. ( 我喜歡你的身材。)

〔'hɛr,staɪl〕 *n.* • my *hairstyle*. ( 我喜歡我的髮型。)

☆ **I like** …和下面的 *want* 一樣，其後都要接自己喜歡的東西，like 的語氣
不如 want 強。如果要強調喜歡的事物時，可以用 very much 來形容，如
*I like you very much.* ( 我非常喜歡你。)另外，如 *I love this book!*
( 我好喜歡這本書！)或 *I love this color* ! ( 我好喜歡這個顏色！)句中，
love 常表程度強烈的「 喜歡 」。請把 I 用 Do you 代替，練習第二人稱疑問
句的說法。

**6** ▲▲▲▲  描述自己希求的慣用語

我想要～
*I want～*

■ 說明想要某種東西 ───────

  • a car.(我想要一輛車。)

  • juice. (我想喝果汁。)

  • coffee. ( 我想喝咖啡。)

■ 說明想有所行動 ───────

  • to go to Disneyland.
    ( 我想去狄斯奈樂園。)

  • to stay here. ( 我想留在這裏。)

〔'tek ə,rɛst〕 • to *take a rest*.(我想休息一下。)

  • to see you again.( 我想再見到你。)

☆想要什麽東西時，**I want** 之後要接 自己所想要的「 物 」；想要有所行動時，
 I want 之後要接不定詞 ( to＋原形動詞)。把句中的 I 換成 Do you 時，就成
 了第二人稱疑問句型，請練習說說看。

## 7

我想～ / 我願意～
## I would like to～

- see you. (我想見你。)
- talk to you. (我想和你談話。)
- invite you to my home.
  (我想邀請你來我家。)
- 〔'haɪkɪŋ〕 *n.* go ***hiking*** with you. (我想和你一起去健行。)
- go driving with you.
  (我想和你一起去開車。)
- have dinner with you.
  (我想和你一起吃晚餐。)
- 〔'kɑpɪ məˈʃin〕 show you how to use this ***copy machine***. (我願意教你用這台影印機。)
- show you how to make this Chinese food. (我願意教你做這道中國菜。)
- say "goodbye." (我想說再見。)
- stay at home today. (我今天想待在家裏。)

☆ **I would like to....** 是 I want to.... 較有禮貌的說法。

## 8

我希望～
## I hope～

- so. (希望如此。)
- you'll be successful. (我希望你會成功。)

● our dreams come true.
( 我希望我們的夢想會實現。)

〔'dʒaɪənt〕 *n.* ● that the **Giants** will win.
( 我希望巨人隊會贏。)

● you will visit me. ( 我希望你來看我。)

● the weather will be fine.
( 我希望天氣轉晴。)

〔'tɜn ‚aʊt〕 ● the picture **turns out** well.
( 我希望照片拍得好看。)

● this rain stops. ( 我希望雨不要再下了。)

● we can get there in time.
( 我希望我們能及時抵達。)

☆ **Hope** 是在願望不確定是否能達成，但希望如此時使用。Hope 後用「 that
子句」表示願望的內容，其中 " that " 可以省略。

# 9 我需要～
## *I need～*

● you. ( 我需要你。)

● your advice. ( 我需要你的建議。)

● time. ( 我需要時間。)

● a vacation. ( 我需要休假。)

● your love. ( 我需要你的愛。)

● your suggestions. ( 我需要你的建議。)

● your help. ( 我需要你的幫助。)

〔'peʃəns〕 *n.* ● *patience*. ( 我需要耐性。)

● more practice. ( 我需要多加練習。)

- a new car.（我需要一部新車。）

- to be careful.（我必須小心行事。）

- something to write with.
  （我需要寫字用具。）

- nice music.（我需要一些好的音樂。）

〔frɛʃ〕*adj.* • to walk in the *fresh* air.
  （我需要在新鮮的空氣裏散步。）

☆ **I need** …是比 I want …溫和的說法。如果改成疑問句時，可有各種表達
方法，如 *Do I need to pay first*?（我得先付錢嗎？）, *Do I need to
stand in line*?（我必須排隊嗎？）, *Do you need my help*?（你需要
我幫忙嗎？）。要注意 Need 之後接動詞時，須用不定詞（ to＋原形動詞）。

▲ ▲ ▲ ▲　描述自己願望的慣用句型

**10**

我期待～／我期望～
# I'm looking forward to~

- seeing you.（我期望見到你。）

- hearing from you.（我期待接到你的信。）

- joining you.（我期待加入你們。）

- driving.（我期待開車。）

- going hiking.（我期望去遠足。）

- going to the movies.
  （我期待去看電影。）

- having dinner with you.
  （我期待和你共進晚餐。）

〔det〕*v.* • *dating*.（我期待約會。）

- spending summer vacation in New
  York.（我期待在紐約過暑假。）

● watching *Back to the Future 2* on
TV　tonight.
（我期待今晚看電視上的「回到未來續集」。）

☆ **I'm looking forward to** …是以愉快的心情期待某件事的意思，是描述自己
的感覺的常用說法。介系詞 to 後面必須接動名詞。I'm waiting.（我在等。）
則是指等待的狀態。

## 11

▲ ▲ ▲ ▲ 　描述自己志願的慣用句型

讓我～
## Let me～

● pay for lunch.（讓我付午餐的錢。）

〔'si ɔf〕 ● *see* you *off* at the airport.
（讓我送你到機場。）

● show you the way.（讓我告訴你怎麼走。）

● try it on.（讓我試穿。）

● answer the telephone.（讓我接電話。）

● drive.（讓我開車。）

● taste it.（讓我嚐嚐。）

● take a rest（讓我休息。）

● see it.（讓我看一下。）

〔'skɛdʒʊl〕 *n.* ● check my *schedule*.（讓我查一下時間表。）

● take your picture.（讓我幫你拍照。）

● try it once again.（讓我再試一次。）

〔ɪk'splen〕 *v.* ● *explain* why I was late.
（讓我解釋遲到的理由。）

- **have time to check it.**
  （讓我有時間檢查。）
- **call him.**（讓我打電話給他。）

☆「**Let me**＋原形動詞」是一種間接命令句型，表「讓我～」。在一般口語中，已沒有什麼命令的含意，反而有種半強制性的請求意味。

▲ ▲ ▲ ▲　描述自己計畫的慣用句型

我應該～

# I'm supposed to~

- **meet him at six.**（我應該六點見他。）
- **go to the bank.**（我應該去銀行。）
- **visit Mr. Stevens tonight.**
  （今晚我應該拜訪史帝芬斯先生。）
- 〔ə'tend〕 *v.* **attend the meeting today.**
  （今晚我應該參加會議。）
- **cook dinner tonight.**（今晚我應該煮晚餐。）
- 〔rɛnt〕 *n.* **pay the rent today.**
  （今天我應該付房租。）
- 〔ˌrikən'fɝm〕 *v.* **reconfirm the flight today.**
  （今天我應該再確認班機。）
- **help Tom move tomorrow.**
  （我明天應該幫湯姆搬家。）

☆ **I'm supposed to** 字面上意思為「我被認為要～」，引申為「我應該～」，可同時傳達「將要」及「必須」兩種語氣，如 *I'm going back to Taipei next week.*（我下週將回台北。）或 *I must go back to Taipei next week.*（我下週必須回台北。）均可說成 *I'm supposed to go back to Taipei next week.* 此外，be not supposed to 也有「應該知道」「說不知道也不行」的語意，如 *In England we are not supposed to play baseball on Sundays.*（在英國星期天是不准打棒球的。）

## 13

▲ ▲ ▲ ▲ 描述自己高興、害怕的慣用句型

我很高興～ / 我很榮幸～
# I'm happy to～/I'm glad to～

- meet you. （我很高興見到你。/幸會！）

- see you again. （我很高興再見到你。）

- hear that. （我很高興聽到那個消息。）

['hɪr frəm] • ***hear from*** you.（我很高興收到你的來信。）

- know you. （我很高興認識你。）

- talk with you. （我很榮幸能和你談話。）

- win the prize. （我很高興得獎。）

['tek ‚pɑrt ɪn] • ***take part in*** this project.
（我很榮幸能參加這項計畫。）

- get this job. （我很高興獲得這份工作。）

[ʃɛr] *v.* • ***share*** this table with you.
（我很高興和你共坐〔分享〕一桌。）

- drive with you.
（我很高興和你一起開車。）

- have a date with you.
（我很高興和你約會。）

- join your program.
（我很高興參加你的計畫。）

☆ **I'm happy to** …和I'm glad to …意思相同。對初次見面的人用 *I'm glad to meet you.* （很高興認識你。），對非初次見面的人則說 *I'm glad to see you.* （很高興見到你。）

# 14

## 我恐怕～ / 我怕～
## *I'm afraid~*

■ **表示遺憾的語氣** ─────────

- I don't speak French.
  （我恐怕不會說法文。）
- I have another appointment.
  （我恐怕有另一個約會。）
- I don't know this area.
  （我恐怕不熟悉這個地方。）
- I can't help you.（我恐怕無法幫助你。）
- I must go right away.
  （我恐怕必須馬上走。）

■ **表示擔心的語氣** ─────────

〔'æksədənt〕*n.*
- of having a car *accident*.
  （我怕出車禍。）
- (I was afraid) that he would die.
  （我怕他會死。）

■ **表示感到害怕、恐怖** ─────────

〔snek〕*n.*
- of *snakes*. （我怕蛇。）
- to go there. （我怕去那裏。）

☆ **I'm afraid** …可用於對談話感到抱歉，或是自己本身恐怕、擔心及不安的時候。由於中文的「對不起」直譯成 I'm sorry.，偶爾也在不必要時使用，但如上例的情形，則使用 I'm afraid …較為適當。如果主詞換掉，如*He was afraid of being late.*（他擔心會遲到。），*Are you afraid of snakes*？（你怕蛇嗎？）等句子也常被使用。I'm not afraid to do…和 I'm not afraid of doing …意思相同。

# 15

表示感動、驚訝的慣用句型

多麼～！／眞～！
## How～！/ What～！

- **How nice!**（眞好！）
- **How expensive this car is!**
  （這部車眞貴！）
- **How loud!**（眞大聲！）
- **How noisy!**（眞吵！）
- 〔'stjupɪd〕 *adj.* **How *stupid* he is!**（他眞笨！）
- **How smart he is!**（他眞聰明！）
- **What a beautiful color!**（多美的顏色啊!）
- **What beautiful stars!**（多美的星星啊！）
- **What a beautiful woman!**
  （多漂亮的女人啊！）
- **What lovely flowers!**（多美的花啊！）
- **What a nice dress!**（多美的衣服啊！）
- 〔rud〕 *adj.* **What a *rude* man!**（多粗魯的人啊！）
- 〔wɛr〕 *v.* **What a nice tie you're *wearing*!**
  （你繫的領帶多美啊！）
- **What a cold morning!**（多冷的早晨啊！）

☆ **What** …！和 **How** …！均用來表示感嘆的語氣，約有下列幾種用法：

- What＋a＋形容詞＋單數可數名詞。如：*What a wonderful view*!（多壯觀啊！）
- What＋形容詞＋不可數名詞/複數名詞。如：*What lovely flowers*!（多可愛的花啊！）
- How＋形容詞，如：*How nice*!（多好啊！）
- How＋形容詞/副詞＋主詞＋動詞，如：*How stupid he is*!（他眞笨！）

以上的 What 與 How 的句型，說起來還是 What 用得比 How 來得多。表示感動和
激動時，還可說 *Oh, no*!（太過份了！）及 *Wonderful*!（太棒了！）等等。

**16** ▲▲ ▲▲ 描述自己感覺的慣用句型

我想～
# I feel like～

- sleeping. （我想睡。）
- being with her. （我想和她在一起。）
- listening to this music. （我想聽這音樂。）
- watching this movie. （我想看這部電影。）
- drinking beer. （我想喝啤酒。）
- taking a walk. （我想散步。）
- staying with you. （我想和你在一起。）

〔kɜɪ〕n. 
- eating *curry* and rice tonight.
  （今晚我想吃咖哩飯。）
- reading this novel. （我想讀這本小說。）

〔ˏhævɪŋ ə ˈdet wɪð〕
- *having a date with* you. （我想和你約會。）

☆ I feel like …和 I like …、I want …類似，都有表達自己慾望的意思。
詢問對方時可用如 *Do you feel like dancing*? （你想跳舞嗎？）等句子。
Feel 之前如果加 don't，表示否定，如 *I don't feel like calling Tom*。
（我不想打電話給湯姆。）

**17** ▲▲ ▲ 描述尋找的慣用句型

我在找～
# I'm looking for～

■ 想找某人時 ────────

- him. （我在找他。）
- my mother. （我在找我的母親。）

■ 想購某物時 ————————

- something colorful.
  （我在找些鮮艷的。）

- something less colorful.
  （我在找些不太鮮艷的。）

- something cheaper.
  （我在找便宜點的東西。）

- a gift.（我在找禮物。）

〔pænts〕 *n.* - *pants.*（我在找褲子。）

- something interesting.
  （我要找點有趣的。）

■ 想找某場所時 ————————

- the post office.（我在找郵局。）

- a hotel.（我在找旅館。）

■ 想找某物時 ————————

〔'wɑlɪt〕 *n.* - my *wallet.*（我在找皮夾。）

〔'sut,kes,'sjut-〕 *n.* - my *suitcase.*（我在找手提箱。）

☆ **I'm looking for** …是在購物時，詢問自己想買的東西時，最常用的說法。想問「附近是否有旅館」時，要說 *I'm looking for a hotel.*（我在找旅館。）詢問別人時則用 *What are you looking for* ?（你在找什麼？）

▲ ▲ ▲ ▲ 詢問對方希求的慣用句型

## 18 你想要～嗎？

# Would you like to～?

- go to a movie?（你想去看電影嗎？）

- see him?（你想見他嗎？）

- have lunch？（你想吃中飯嗎？）
- sit down？（你想坐下來嗎？）
- go there？（你想去那兒嗎？）
- buy this？（你想買這個嗎？）
- have some coffee？（你想喝些咖啡嗎？）
- dance with me？（你想和我一起跳舞嗎？）
- join us？（你想加入我們嗎？）

☆ **Would you like to** …？（你想要～嗎？）和 **_Do you want to_** …？意思相同，但前者比較禮貌些。想詢問對方的想法及願望時，可用此一基本句型。不過，_Would you show me the way to the hospital_？（請告訴我醫院怎麼走。）如果說成 _Would you like to show me the way to the hospital_？則語意會變成「你是不是想告訴我醫院怎麼走？」。須注意此差別，以免造成誤解。

# 19

你喜歡～嗎？
## _Do you like～?_

- him？（你喜歡他嗎？）
- movies？（你喜歡電影嗎？）
〔'suʃɪ〕*n.* • **_sushi_**？（你喜歡壽司嗎？）
- this red shirt？（你喜歡這件紅襯衫嗎？）
- this or that？（你喜歡這個還是那個？）
- studying Chinese？（你喜歡學中文嗎？）
- traveling？（你喜歡旅行嗎？）
- climbing mountains？（你喜歡爬山嗎？）

- sports？（你喜歡運動嗎？）

- watching sports？（你喜歡看運動比賽嗎?）

☆ **Like** 之後要接所欲問的東西（受詞）。如果純粹問喜不喜歡車子，說 Do you like cars？即可，如果是問喜不喜歡開車的行動，則要用動名詞 driving，說成 Do you like driving？

# 20

## ～如何？／～怎麼樣？
# How about～？

- a drink？（喝杯飲料如何？）

- coffee？（喝杯咖啡如何？）

- you？（你呢？）

〔kən'sʌlt〕 *v.* - ***consult**ing the dictionary*？
（查查字典如何？）

- asking him for directions？
（向他問路怎麼樣？）

- joining us？（加入我們怎麼樣？）

- seeing a doctor？（去看醫生怎麼樣？）

- taking a walk？（散散步怎麼樣？）

〔'jogɑ〕 *n.* - practicing *yoga* with me？
（和我一起練瑜珈怎麼樣？）

〔'pʌblɪk,bæθ〕 - going to the ***public bath***？
（去澡堂洗澡如何?）

- trying on this dress？
（要不要試穿這件衣服？）

- taking a break？（休息一下如何？）
- going out for dinner？
  （出去吃晚餐如何？））

☆ 想問「～如何？」時應該立刻想到 **How about** …？不過 How about 之後接名詞或動名詞要注意。可用 *We're going to see a movie. How about you*？（我們要去看電影，你呢？）。另外也有用法類似，但稍有差別的 What about you？。What about you？是詢問對方意見的用法。

# 21　咱們～吧！ Let's～!

## ■ Go的說法

- go.（咱們走吧！）
- go home, shall we？
  （咱們回家吧，好嗎？）
- go out driving.（咱們去開車吧！）
- go shopping.（咱們去逛街吧！）
- go see a movie together.
  （咱們一起去看電影吧！）

## ■ Take的說法

- take a break.（咱們休息一下吧！）
- take a rest.（咱們休息一下吧！）
- take a little walk.（咱們去散步吧！）

## ■ Have的說法

- have a talk in my room.
  （咱們在我房間聊聊天吧！）

- have a beer or something.
  （咱們喝點啤酒什麼的！）

- have a conversation. （咱們談談天吧！）

〔rɪˈhɜsḷ〕 *n.* • have a *rehearsal*. （咱們預演一下吧！）

- have a drink.（咱們喝點飲料吧！）

## ■ Make的說法 ─────────

- make it five. （咱們約五點見吧！）

- make coffee. （咱們來泡咖啡吧！）

- make something to eat.
  （咱們煮些東西來吃吧！）

## ■ Get的說法 ─────────

- get something to eat.
  （咱們找點東西來吃吧！）

- get together for lunch.
  （咱們一起吃午飯吧！）

- get out and walk for a while.
  （咱們出去散散步吧！）

## ■ 其他 ─────────

- eat out tonight. （咱們今晚出去吃吧！）

- keep in touch. （咱們保持連絡吧！）

- change the subject.（咱們換個話題吧！）

- play tennis. （咱們去打網球吧！）

〔ˈsæləd〕 *n.* • share a *salad*. （咱們共吃一份沙拉吧！）

- walk to your hotel.（咱們走去你的飯店吧！）

☆ **Let** 和 **have**, **make** 在文法上都被稱爲「使役動詞」，Let's 是 let us 的縮寫，在口語中表勸誘或提議。使役動詞的 let 和 make、see、hear 一樣，不需要不定詞 to，後面直接加原形動詞即可。

# 22

為什麼不~？
# Why don't~?

- you buy these pants?
  （你為什麼不買這些褲子？）

- we see this movie?
  （我們為什麼不看這部電影呢？）

〔,hæv ə'sit〕 • you ***have a seat***?（為什麼你不坐下來呢？）

- you have a piece of this cake?
  （你為什麼不吃一片蛋糕？）

〔,ɪntrə'djus〕 *v.* • you ***introduce*** her to me?
  （你為什麼不把她介紹給我？）

- you marry her?（你為什麼不和她結婚？）

- you ask a policeman?
  （你為什麼不去問警察？）

〔'sɛpərɪtlɪ〕 *adv.* • we pay the bill ***separately***?
  （我們為什麼不分開付帳？）

☆ 以 **Why don't** …？起首的句子中有建議、不滿或抱怨之含意。而第一例句中
的 Why don't you …？因有建議的意思，所以又可以說成 I suggest that…。

# 23

我建議~
# I suggest (that)~

- you go to see a doctor.
  （我建議你去看醫生。）

- you buy a new one.
  （我建議你買個新的。）

〔əˈkaʊnt〕 *n.* • you open a bank *account* first.
  （我建議你先在銀行裏開一個戶頭。）

- you write your name first.
  （我建議你先寫名字。）

- you be careful not to catch cold.
  （我建議你小心別感冒了。）

- you watch your step.
  （我建議你走路小心。）

- you get a job with that company.
  （我建議你到那家公司找工作。）

- you study Chinese. （我建議你去學中文。）

- you take a taxi. （我建議你搭計程車。）

☆ **I suggest that** … （我建議～。）意思同於 *I want you to* … （我要你～。），前者語氣上委婉得多。想將自己的意見傳達給對方時，這是很好用的句型。但是，*I suggest that you see a doctor.* （我建議你去看醫生。）不可以說成 I suggest you to see a doctor. 切記。

# 24 徵求對方同意的慣用句型
## 你介意～嗎？
## *Do you mind~?*

- my smoking？（你介意我抽煙嗎？）

- if I smoke？（你介意我抽煙嗎？）

- sharing the table？
  （你介意我和你共用桌子嗎？）

- if I sit next to you？
  （你介意我坐你旁邊嗎？）

- helping me？（你介意幫我一個忙嗎？）
- opening the window？
  （你介意把窗戶打開嗎？）

☆ **Do you mind** … ? 是用於詢問對方意見，語氣較一般疑問句謙恭，也可問成
**Would you mind** … ? 回答這種疑問句要特別小心，如有人問 *Do you mind*
*opening the window*?（你介意把窗戶打開嗎？），不希望開窗時，要回答
*Yes.*（*I mind* opening the window.）；反之，如果不介意開窗，就回答No.
（*I don't mind* opening the window.）

## 我能～嗎？
# May I～?/Can I～?

■ **想取得對方許可** ────────

- use this telephone？（我能用這部電話嗎?）
- use your bathroom？（我能用你的浴室嗎?）
- smoke？（我可以抽煙嗎？）

■ **提出建議** ────────

- help you？（我能幫你什麼忙嗎？）
- open the window？（我能把窗戶打開嗎？）
〔bro'ʃʊr, -'ʃjʊr〕*n.* • have this ***brochure***？
  （我能借一下這本小冊子嗎？）

☆ **May I** … ?（我可以～嗎？）與 ***Can I*** … ?（我能～嗎？）意思相近。而說
*May I use this telephone*?（我可以借用一下電話嗎？）要比說 *Can I*
*use this telephone*?（我用一下電話好嗎？）有禮貌些。*May I help you*?
原意是「需要我幫忙嗎？」，但在某些場合，如對迷路的人也可以這麼問，
以表示友好及關懷。

## 26

對對方有所要求的慣用句型

### 你能～嗎？
# Would you～?

- **tell me your phone number？**
  （你能告訴我你的電話號碼嗎？）

- **show me that camera？**
  （你能讓我看一下那台照相機嗎？）

〔͵gɪv ə ˈlɪft〕 • ***give** me **a lift** to my house？*
  （你能送我回家嗎？）

〔͵gɪv ə ˈrɪŋ〕 • ***give** me **a ring** tomorrow？*
  （你明天能打電話給我嗎？）

- **open the window？**（你能開一下窗戶嗎？）

- **take me to the hospital？**
  （你能送我去醫院嗎？）

- **introduce her？**（你能不能介紹她一下？）

☆ **Would you** …？ 是 Will you …? 較客氣的說法，表謙恭的請求。希望對方做某件事時，儘量用 Would you …? 等較客氣的用法。

## 27

詢問對方喜好的慣用句型

### 你比較喜歡A，還是B？
# Which do you like better, A or B?

■ 詢問對食物的喜好 ─────────

- **coffee or black tea？**
  （你比較喜歡咖啡還是紅茶？）

- **Chinese food or Japanese food？**
  （你比較喜歡中國菜還是日本料理？）

- bread or rice？（你比較喜歡麵包還是飯？）
- beer or juice？（你比較喜歡啤酒還是果汁？）
- red wine or white wine？
  （你比較喜歡紅酒還是白酒？）

〔'sʌnɪ ,saɪd ʌp〕
〔'skræmbḷd〕 *adj.*
- ***sunny-side up*** or ***scrambled*** ?
  （你比較喜歡荷包蛋還是炒蛋？）

■ 詢問對電影、音樂的喜好 ────────

- rock or classical music ?
  （你比較喜歡搖滾樂還是古典音樂?）

〔'kɑmədɪz〕*n.*
- ***comedies*** or love stories ?
  （你比較喜歡喜劇片還是文藝片？）

■ 詢問對運動的喜好 ────────

- summer sports or winter sports?
  （你比較喜歡夏天的運動還是冬天的運動？）

■ 其他 ────────

- blue or red?（你比較喜歡藍色還是紅色？）
- this or that?（你比較喜歡這個還是那個?）

☆ **Which do you like better, A or B**? 與 **Do you like A or B**? 意思相近，
被問的人均回答 A 或 B 就對了。唯前句語意著重在詢問對方「比較」喜歡哪
一個，後一句則純粹問喜歡與否。

哪種～？
# *What kind of～?*

- music do you like ?（你喜歡哪種音樂?）
- drink do you want?（你要哪種飲料？）

- movies do you like？（你喜歡哪種電影？）
- flower is this？（這是哪種花？）
- food do you like？（你喜歡哪種食物？）

☆ **kind of** 是指事物的種類。如 *I'm not the kind of man that would take advantage of you*. ( 我不是那種會利用你的人 )。又如：What kind of music, 問的是搖滾、 流行、或古典等音樂種類；What kind of drink, 問的是啤酒、葡萄酒、威士忌等的酒類；What kind of movies, 問的是喜劇片、恐怖片、動作片、文藝愛情片等的電影種類。

## 29

使用感官動詞的慣用句型

聽起來～

# *It sounds~*

- interesting. ( 聽起來很有趣。)
- funny. ( 聽起來很滑稽。)
- wonderful. ( 聽起來很棒。)
- unusual. ( 聽起來很不尋常。)
- stupid. ( 聽起來很愚蠢。)

[ˈsɪlɪ] *adj.*
- *silly*. ( 聽起來很愚蠢。)
- like a good idea. ( 聽起來似乎是個好主意。)
- like it might be fun.
  ( 聽起來可能很好玩。)
- like you have a cold.
  ( 聽起來你好像感冒了。)
- like you enjoyed it.
  ( 聽起來你好像蠻喜歡的。)

■ 用**You**當主詞的說法 ─────────

〔dɪ'prɛst〕 *adj*. ● （You）sound *depressed*.
（你聽起來似乎很沮喪。）

● （You）sound happy.
（你聽起來似乎很快樂。）

● He sounds like an American.
（他聽起來像是個美國人。）

☆ 美國人寫信時或交談時，常用 It sounds 的句型。如回信時常寫*Well，it sounds like you had a very nice vacation.*（你似乎過了個快樂的假期。）You sound …則常用在電話對談中，當然，面對面時也可以說。

# 30 好像～
# *It seems～*

● to me that he likes drinking.
（我覺得他好像喜歡喝酒。）

● to me that he wants a Japanese girl friend.
（我覺得他好像想交個日本女朋友。）

● to me that he would like to go back home.（我覺得他好像想要回家。）

● to me that we need more discussion about that.
（我覺得我們似乎需要多討論那件事。）

〔'sɛlfɪʃ〕 *adj*. ● to me that he is *selfish*.
（我覺得他好像很自私。）

〔'sɛnsətɪv〕 *adj*. ● to me that she is *sensitive*.
（我覺得她好像很敏感。）

■ 用 **You** 當主詞時的說法 ─────────

- （You） seem  angry.（你好像很生氣。）
- （You） seem  very  happy.
  （你好像十分快樂。）
- （You） seem  nervous.（你好像很緊張。）

〔ʃaɪ〕 *adj.*
- （You） seem  *shy*.（你好像很害羞。）
- （You） seem  sad.（你好像很悲傷。）

〔'sɪŋgḷ〕 *adj.*
- （You） seem  to  be  *single*.
  （你好像是單身。）

■ 用第三人稱時的說法 ─────────

- （He） seems  to  be  a  German.
  （他好像是德國人。）
- （He） seems  to  be  intelligent.
  （他好像很聰明。）
- （He） seems  to  be  a  doctor.
  （他好像是位醫生。）
- （He） seems  to  be  ill.
  （他好像生病了。）
- （He） seems  to  have  caught  a  cold.
  （他好像感冒了。）

〔twɪn〕 *n.*
- （They） seem  to  be  *twins*.
  （他們好像是雙胞胎。）
- （They） seem  to  be  brothers.
  （他們好像是兄弟。）

☆ **It seems to me that** …（我覺得～。）是「It … that …」的句型，同於 *I think* …。that 後面，接上自己所認為的事物即可。而 *He seems to like drinking.*（他好像很喜歡喝酒。）雖與 *I think he likes drinking.* 意思相同，但 He seems to 的語氣顯得較有根據。陳述同一件事，若會兩種說法，會話能力將大幅擴增。

**31**

看起來～
*It looks～*

- very nice.（看起來很漂亮。）
- like a bird.（看起來像隻鳥。）

〔mæn'hætn〕*n.*
- like *Manhattan*.（看起來像是曼哈頓。）
- like a picture.（看起來像幅畫。）
- like a lot of fun.（看起來好像很有趣。）
- as if it's going to rain.
  （看起來像要下雨了。）

〔'latərɪ〕*n.*
- (You) look as if you already won the *lottery*.
  （你看起來好像已經中了獎券似的。）
- (You) look very much like your mother.（你看起來很像你母親。）
- (You) look angry.（你看起來很生氣。）

〔'æktrɪs〕*n.*
- (You) look like an *actress*.
  （你看起來像是個女演員。）
- (You) look like a movie star.
  （你看起來像是電影明星。）
- (You) look like Paul Newman.
  （你看起來像保羅‧紐曼。）

〔'wʌndəfəl〕*adj.*
- (You) look *wonderful*.
  （你看起來很漂亮。）
- (You) look like you're having a good time tonight.
  （你看起來好像今晚玩得挺愉快的。）

- （You）look like someone I know.
  （你看起來好像我認識的一個人。）

- （He）looks his age.
  （他看起來和他的年紀相符。）

- （He）looks like his mother.
  （他看起來像他母親。）

- （The house）looks so beautiful.
  （這棟房子看起來很漂亮。）

☆ seem 是經由周圍氣氛或其他感覺所下的判斷，**look** 則是經由眼睛觀察後產生的判斷，如 *You look very nice.*（你看起來很美/很帥。）look 之後要接形容詞，如 *It looks nice.*（看起來很漂亮。）look like 後要接名詞，如 *It looks like a bird.*（看起來像一隻鳥。）look as if 後接子句，如 *It looks as if it's going to rain.*（看起來好像要下雨了。）

## 32 我聽說～
## I heard～

- that you'll be going back to your country. Is that true?
  （我聽說你要回國了，是眞的嗎？）

- that your wife is sick. Is she OK?
  （聽說你太太生病了，她還好嗎？）

- that you have something to tell me. What is it?
  （聽說你有事要告訴我，到底是什麼？）

〔'mɪd,naɪt〕 *n.*
- a strange sound at *midnight*. How about you?
  （我半夜聽到奇怪的聲音，你有沒有聽到？）

〔‚prizɛn'teʃən〕 *n.* ● that your ***presentation*** was accepted.
Congratulations!

（我聽說你的報告被接受了，恭喜恭喜！）

〔kən‚grætʃə'leʃənz〕 *n.* ● that you're getting married. ***Congratulations***!

（聽說你要結婚了，恭喜恭喜！）

● that you like Chinese food.

（聽說你喜歡吃中國菜。）

〔'ɝθ‚kwek〕 *n.* ● there was a big ***earthquake*** in San Francisco.（聽說舊金山發生大地震。）

● you're a fan of John Wayne.

（聽說你是約翰韋恩的影迷。）

● you're an admirer of Elvis.

（聽說你是艾維斯〔貓王〕的仰慕者。）

● our flight will be delayed two hours. Is that right?

（聽說我們的飛機將延誤兩小時，是眞的嗎？）

〔'sʌb‚we〕 *n.* ● that there is no ***subway*** in Los Angeles.（聽說洛杉磯沒有地下鐵。）

● that you passed the examination. Congratulations!

（聽說你通過考試了，恭喜恭喜！）

〔straɪk〕 *n.* ● the ***strike*** was ***called off***. Is that
〔'kɔl ɔf〕 right?（聽說罷工取消了，是眞的嗎？）

● you had a baby. Congratulations!

（聽說你懷孕了，恭喜恭喜！）

ㄥ **Hear** 是感官動詞，和 ***smell***、***feel***、***taste*** 一樣，沒有現在進行式。如：
I'm hearing somebody coming. 就是錯誤的句子。I hear 後面的 that
可省略。I heard 並不一定指實際聽到的事情，由信上得知的事也可用 I
heard，如：*I heard you had moved to Los Angeles.*（聽說你搬去洛
杉磯了。）

# 33

聞起來～
## *It smells～*

- good.（聞起來很香。）

- bad.（聞起來很臭。）

- （You）smell beautiful.
  （你聞起來好香。）

- （Can you）smell something burning?
  （你有沒有聞到燒焦味？）

- （Something）smells like roses.
  （聞起來像玫瑰花的東西。）

- （That）smells funny. What's in it?
  （那個味道很奇怪，裏面是什麼？）

# 34

我知道～
## *I see～*

- what you want to say.
  （我知道你想說什麼。）

- what you mean.
  （我了解你的意思。）

- what you want.（我知道你要什麼。）

- he is right.（我知道他是對的。）

- they did so.（我知道他們這樣做。）

- the story is true.
  （ 我知道這故事是眞的。）

- you are right. （ 我知道你是對的。）

☆ **I see** 有「看到」( look) 及「了解」(understand) 兩個含意，如：*You have to pay first.*（ 請先付帳。）/ *I see.* （ 知道了。）也可反問對方 *You see?* （ 懂嗎？）。此外，see 還有 meet 的含意，如 *I'm seeing my client at three o'clock.*（ 3 點時我有客人要來。）

# 35

謝謝你～
# Thank you for～

表示謝意的慣用句型

- giving me a lift. （謝謝你讓我搭便車。）
- your good advice. （ 謝謝你的忠告。）
- calling. （ 謝謝你打電話來。）
- your help. （ 謝謝你的幫忙。）
- your letter. （ 謝謝你寫信來。）

〔'vɪdɪo 'tep〕
- lending me the *video tape*.
  （ 謝謝你借我錄影帶。）

- sending me so many things.
  （ 謝謝你送我這麼多東西。）

- introducing her to me.
  （ 謝謝你把她介紹給我。）

☆ 英語中感謝的說法有很多種，如下面例子：
I would like to say " thank you ".
I have to say " thank you. "
Finally I should say " thank you " again.
I appreciate your kindness.
I appreciate the fact that you taught me English.
Thank you 是口語上表達謝意用的，而 I appreciate 則是書面的感謝用語。

# 36

### 誰～?
# Who～?

- is calling？（誰？）
- is it？（誰？）
- is he？（他是誰？）
- are you calling？（你打電話給誰？）
- are you looking for？（你找誰？）
- are you going with？（你和誰一起去？）

〔'fevərɪt〕 *adj.* 
- is your *favorite* movie star？
（你最喜歡的電影明星是誰？）

〔ə'hɛd〕 *adv.* 
- is *ahead*？（誰贏了？）
- is your boss？（你的老板是誰？）
- knows it？（誰知道？）
- （With）whom do you live?
（你和誰住在一起？）

☆ 當問起「是誰～」或「和誰～」時，可以說以 **Who** 開頭的句子。不過，當面對面時，直接問對方 Who are you？是很失禮的，就如同在問對方「喂！你到底是誰啊？」一樣。像這種時候，想知道對方是誰時，可說 *May I ask your name*？

# 37

### ～在哪兒?
# Where～?

- is your office？（你辦公室在哪兒？）
- are you going？（你要去哪兒？）

　〔hɛd〕 v. ● are you **head**ing？（你要去哪兒？）

　　　　　● do you live？（你住哪兒？）

　　　　　● have you been these days？
　　　　　（這幾天你去哪兒了？）

　　　　　● have you been this summer？
　　　　　（今年夏天你去了哪裏？）

　　　　　● will you stay tonight？（今晚你要待在哪裏？）

〔'nɛk, taɪ〕 n. ● did you buy that **necktie**？
　　　　　（你那條領帶在哪兒買的？）

　　　　　● were you born？（你在哪裏出生？）

〔'drɑp ɔf〕　● should I **drop** you **off**？
　　　　　（我該讓你在哪裏下車？）

　　　　　● shall we have lunch？
　　　　　（我們要去哪裏吃午餐？）

　　　　　● will you meet her？（你和她要在哪裏碰面？）

　　　　　● do you usually buy your food？
　　　　　（你通常在哪裏買食物？）

☆ 使用 who 以外的疑問詞如 Where …？等時，注意動詞或助動詞要放在主詞之前。

# 38 什麼？
# What～?

　　　　　● brought you here？（什麼風把你吹來的？）

　　　　　● do you have in mind？（你心裏在想什麼？）

　　　　　● are you thinking about？（你在想什麼？）

　　　　　● time will you be back today？
　　　　　（今天你幾時要回來？）

- time should I call you tonight?
  （我今天晚上該幾點打電話給你？）

- number are you calling? You have the wrong number.
  （你打幾號？你打錯了。）

- did he say?（他說些什麼？）

- did you say?（你說什麼？）

- do you mean by that?
  （你說那話是什麼意思？）

- are you doing here?（你在這裏做什麼？）

- were you doing there yesterday?
  （昨天你在那裏做什麼？）

- time will you be there?
  （你幾時會在那裏？）

- time can you come over?
  （你幾時過來？）

- time shall I come over?
  （我要什麼時候過來？）

- time will the show start?
  （表演幾時開始？）

- time will the party be over?
  （宴會幾時結束？）

- time will we leave here?
  （我們幾時離開這兒？）

- would you like to drink?
  （你想喝什麼？）

- would you like to eat?
  （你想吃什麼？）

- material is it made of?
  （這是用什麼做成的？）

- kind of Chinese food do you like best?（你最喜歡哪種中國菜？）

- is happening？（什麼事？）

- happened？（怎麼了？）

- made you so angry？
  （你為什麼事生這麼大的氣？）

- can I do for you？
  （我可以幫你做什麼嗎？）

☆ **What brought you here**？字面上意思是「什麼風把你吹來的？」而 Why did you come here？雖然意思和上句相同，但其隱藏在後的含意却是「你為什麼來這裏？你不可以來的。」

# 39

## 我與～無關
## *I have nothing to do with～*

■ **以自己爲主詞時** ────────

- you.（我和你沒什麼關係。）

〔'ɛnɪmɔr〕*adv.* • him **anymore**.（我跟他不再有什麼瓜葛了。）

- the ABC Company.
  （我和ＡＢＣ公司沒什麼關係。）

- this matter.（我和這件事無關。）

■ **以過去式表示時** ────────

- （I had nothing to do with）that car accident.
  （我和那場車禍沒有關係。）

■ 第三人稱的說法 ─────────

> ● (He has nothing to do with) this
>   project. (他和這項計畫沒有關係。)

〔'prɛgnənsɪ〕 *n.* ● (He has nothing to do with) her
>   ***pregnancy***. (他跟她懷孕沒有關係。)

☆ **Have nothing to do with** … (與～無關)是慣用片語，而要說明「與～有
關」就用 have someing to do with … ，如：I think the trouble with
the copy machine *has something to do with* the mechanism for
moving the paper.(我認為影印機故障的原因與輸送紙張的部分有關。)

## 40　有～
# *There is～/There are～*

> ● a post office behind this building.
>   (這棟建築物後面有間郵局。)

〔pə'lis bɑks〕 ● a ***police box*** along this street.
>   (沿這條街有一間派出所。)

> ● a station around that corner.
>   (在那個轉角處有個車站。)

〔rɪ'frɪdʒə,retɚ〕 *n.* ● something cold in the ***refrigerator***.
>   (冰箱裏有些冰的東西。)

〔'bekərɪ〕 *n.* ● a ***bakery*** about ten meters away.
>   (大概十公尺外有家麵包店。)

〔'steʃən,ɛrɪ〕 *n.* ● a ***stationery*** shop down this street.
>   (這條街上有家文具店。)

## ■ 複數的用法 ——————

- （There are）coffee cups in the kitchen.（廚房裏有些咖啡杯。）

〔ˈkʌbəd〕 *n.*
- （There are）tea cups in the *cupboard*.（碗櫥裏有些茶杯。）

☆ 當提及與說話者有一段距離的事物時，我們可以使用 " **there** " 來說明。指與說話者同一場所的事物，則用 " **here** " ，如：*Here is my book.*（我的書在這兒）；*There comes the bus.*（公車來了。）。另外，當我們在國外看到戶外的指示地圖時，上面的 " 現在位置 " 就是寫成 "*You are here.* " 還有，由電話對談中我們也可以了解 here 和 there 的差別，如：" *Is Tom there*？ "（Tom 在不在那裏？）" No. He is not here."（不，他不在這裏。）

# 附錄 I：練習題參考答案

## 第 16、17 頁

(1) Professor Brown？（ ↗ ）（ OR Excuse me, Professor Brown？
( ↗ )；OR Good afternoon, Professor Brown.）

(2) Tom！（OR Hey, Tom！；OR Watch out, Tom！；OR Hey, kid！）

(3) Excuse me.（OR Sorry to bother you, but....）

(4) Excuse me, sir？（ ↗ ）（ OR Oh, sir？（ ↗ ）；OR Good
afternoon, sir.）

(5) Steve？（ ↗ ）（ OR Excuse me, Steve？）

(6) Pardon me.（OR Excuse me.；OR Excuse me, miss.）

## 第 32、33 頁

(1) Hi！I'm Jane Smith.

(2) Hello！It's good to see you again.

(3) How do you like Montreal？

(4) Do you like jazz？

(5) What is the best way to travel in New Jersey？

(6) Excuse me, sir. Can you recommend a good book on films？

(7) Let's get started with today's program.

(8) Those are stylish pants.

## 第 44、45 頁

(1) (i) I'm getting a little confused.

(ii) Would you speak more slowly？（OR Would you repeat
that？）

(2) I fail to see the point.（ OR I'm not following you.）

(3) (i) Would you repeat the train information ?

  (ii) Pardon ? ( OR Excuse me ? ; I beg your pardon ? )

(4) I didn't understand what you said. ( OR I didn't hear you.)

(5) (i) I am saying that

  (ii) Didn't I tell you ? ( OR Don't you remember ? )

(6) No, I said Perry.

(7) Let me repeat the instructions. ( OR Let's review the instructions.)

## 第 56、57 頁

(1) (i) I'm not sure I follow you.

  (ii) Is that clear ? ( OR Do you follow me ? )

  (iii) You mean

(2) (i) Do you mean

  (ii) I meant that ( OR What I meant was)

(3) Are you sure ?

(4) (i) I was (clearly) misquoted.

  (ii) What I said was ( OR I said)

## 第 65、66 頁

(1) A : Can you explain a little bit more ?

  B : What do you mean ?

(2) Would you elaborate ( on that) ?

(3) What's the meaning of " plant "? ( OR " Plant " ? )

(4) For example ? ( OR For instance ? ; Like what ? )

(5) Why are you asking me that ?

(6) What I meant was that ( OR By that I meant )

## 第 78、79 頁

### PART I

(1) To be honest with you

(2) as a rule

(3) In many cases

### PART II

(1) That's more or less true, but I think she looks good in any color.

(2) I see what you mean, but some people don't want to live with " one person " their entire lives.

(3) Well, I don't know, but the weather report I always listen to is pretty accurate.

## 第 86、87 頁

### PART I

(1) Um.... Well.... I'm uh....

(2) Well, see, uh.... the thing is... I....

(3) Well, look, uh... I would love to, but uh... you know....

(4) Uh, well, look... I meant... you know....

### PART II

(1) Oh, I meant

(2) Oh, pardon me, I meant

## 第 100、101 頁

(1) You know what？(OR Guess what.)

(2) You know what？(OR Guess what.)

(3) Tell you what. (OR I'll tell you what.; OR How about this?)

(4) How about this? ( OR How does this sound? )

(5) How about this? (OR How does this sound?; OR What do you think of this? ; OR I know what we can do.; OR How about this?)

(6) By the way

(7) Anyway

## 第 108、109 頁

(1) B : Excuse me for interrupting, but could you move two seats over ? You are sitting in our seats.
   A : Oh ! We are sorry.

(2) B : Pardon me. I couldn't help overhearing you. Did you say you're from Now York?
   A : Yes, that's right. Are you from New York, too?

(3) B : Wait a second! I didn't know that!!
   A : I didn't know either until I got this postcard from them.

(4) B : Excuse me, Bob. Can I ask you a question?
   ( OR Can I say something?)
   A : Sure, go ahead.

(5) B : Sorry, but why do they call it "Florence"?
   A : I don't know. And why is it a female name?

(6) B : Hold it, Tom. Did you say Doris ?
   A : Yes. She's leaving tomorrow. Don't you know that ?

## 第 122、123 頁

PART I

(1) (a) A plane crash in Germany?! ( ↗ )
   (b) Really ?
   (c) Oh my God ! How terrible!
   (d) Oh, I'm sorry to hear that.

(2) (a) It's cancelled?! ( ↗ ) ( OR Oh no! )

   (b) That's disappointing.

   (c) Oh, shoot!

   (d) That's too bad.

(3) (a) They're getting married?! ( ↗ )

   (b) You are kidding.

   (c) That's great! I'm happy for them!

   (d) Oh yeah? When?

(4) (a) John is going to be the next President?! ( ↗ )

   (b) Oh yeah? ( ↗ )

   (c) So what? ( ↘ )

   (d) And, William is going to be the next Vice President!

## PART II

(1) If I may add a word

(2) And, on top of that

## 第 129 頁

(1) A: It's been great seeing you again.

   B: Same here.

   A: Please keep in touch. Good friends are hard to find.

   B: Sure I will. And you too.

   A: Take care.

(2) A: My phone bill is going to be very high. I'd better hang up.

   B: I forgot you were calling long distance. I'll let you go now.

   A: It's been nice talking with you.

   B: Yes, I've enjoyed talking with you.

   A: I'll be thinking of you. Bye.

   B: Bye now.

(3) A : I'm sorry to have taken up so much of your time. I'd better
       let you go.

　　 B : It's been a pleasure talking with you.

　　 A : I'll call you again.

　　 B : Yes, please. And I'll call you, too.

　　 A : So long.

　　 B : So long.

(4) A : Let's get together sometime.

　　 B : That will be nice.

　　 A : Well, I'll talk to you soon.

　　 B : Okay. Take it easy.

　　 A : Good night.

　　 B : Good night.

# 附錄 Ⅱ：練習題中文翻譯（含答案）

## 第 *1* 章

1. 對布朗教授

    A：布朗教授？（或：打擾一下，布朗教授？）（或：午安，布朗教授。）

    B：嗨，湯姆，有需要我幫忙的地方嗎？

    A：我很擔心我的成績，你能推薦一位家教給我嗎？

    B：別擔心，我會幫你的。

2. 對一個小男孩，你知道他叫湯姆

    A：湯姆！（或：嗨，湯姆！）（或：小心，湯姆！）（或：嗨，小子！）

    B：幹嘛？

    A：你小心點，不然會傷到自己。

    B：我喜歡在電梯裏玩。

    A：我曉得，但是如果你繼續玩，就會跌倒，所以趕快停下來。

    B：好吧！

3. 對宴會中的陌生人

    A：對不起，（或：抱歉打擾你，…）你是比爾‧海斯嗎？

    B：不，我是比爾‧梅斯。

    A：我以為你姓海斯。

    B：不，是梅斯。你叫什麼名字？

    A：波里。

    B：哦，我以為你叫郝利呢！

    A&B：無論如何，很高興見到你！

4. 對店裡的人

    A：對不起，先生？（或：哦，先生？）（或：午安，先生。）

    B：嗯，有什麼我可以效勞的？

    A：有，我能和店經理談一談嗎？

B：我就是經理。

A：太好了！我想要介紹給你這一系列新款式的衣服。

5. 對你的工作夥伴，史提夫

A：史提夫？（或：打擾一下，史提夫？）

B：什麼事？

A：我能問你一個問題嗎？

B：當然囉，我不介意。

A：你那件夾克是在哪兒買的？

6. 對接待員

A：對不起（或：打擾一下）（或：打擾一下，小姐），請問失物招領
　　處在哪兒？

B：沿著走廊走，經過六個門後，向左轉，再向右轉，它就在你眼前了。

A：有比較近的路嗎？

B：抱歉，恐怕沒有。

## 第 *2* 章

1. 在宴會中

A：嗨！我叫珍·史密斯。

B：嗨！我叫山姆·伯金斯。

A：你喜歡這個宴會嗎？

B：喜歡，感覺真的很棒。

2. 在辦公室裏

A：哈囉！再見到你真好。

B：嗨，很抱歉我不記得你。

A：抱歉，我叫約瑟夫，我們去年在學校見過面。

B：哦，對！沒錯！我很抱歉，我的記性不好。

A：沒關係，真高興見到你。

3. 在蒙特利爾附近的火車上

　　A：你覺得蒙特利爾如何？

　　B：那裏很美。

　　A：我想你也會喜歡巴黎。

　　B：是的，事實上，我曾住過那裏，也喜歡那裏。

4. 在酒店裏、欣賞爵士樂

　　A：你喜歡爵士樂嗎？

　　B：喜歡，你最喜歡的歌手是哪位？

　　A：我沒有最喜歡的，不過我喜歡爵士樂中的薩克斯風手。

　　B：我喜歡橫笛。

5. 在遊客詢問臺

　　A：到紐澤西旅行的最好方法是什麼？

　　B：嗯，理想的狀況是，最好有部車。

　　A：我沒有車。

　　B：次好的運輸工具是公車，又便宜又快。

6. 在書店

　　A：對不起，先生，你能否推薦一本關於電影的好書？

　　B：你對電影的哪方面有興趣？

　　A：我想看關於導演的。

　　B：你應該看霍華德・史密斯寫的「好萊塢電影導演」，它放在第四排。

7. 在會議中

　　A：我們來開始今天的議題。

　　B：等一下，有一位發言者還沒到。

　　A：誰沒來？

　　B：史特林先生。

8. 在朋友家

    A： 這褲子很時髦。

    B： 哦，謝謝，你這樣說真好心。

    A： 我是說真的。

    B： 我知道，我也很喜歡。


# 第 *3* 章

1. A： (i)我有點搞迷糊了。

    B： 你哪裏搞迷糊了？

    A： 我不懂你對如何去博物館的指示，(ii)你能不能說慢一點？（或：你能否再說一次？）

    B： 好的，搭這班火車到第九十六街，然後再換第D車。


2. A： 我不知道重點是什麼（或：我好像沒聽懂你說的），你想要說什麼？

    B： 重點就是我們應該立刻開始。


3. A： 車掌，(i)你能否重覆一下這班車的情形？

    B： 好的，這班車誤點了，請改搭慢車。

    A： 那班車能載我去賓州車站嗎？

    B： (ii)你說什麼？（或：對不起？）（或：請你再說一次，好嗎？）

    A： 那班慢車有到賓州車站嗎？

    B： 哦，會的。


4. A： 很抱歉，我不懂你在說什麼（或：我聽不到）。

    B： 我是說：「電影下午三點半開演。」


5. A： 我不知道你在說什麼。

    B： (i)我是說你應該去醫院。

    A： 我臉色很差嗎？

    B： 不是！(ii)我沒告訴你嗎？（或：你不記得嗎？）你該去那兒看你妹妹。

6. A：嗨，我叫派瑞。

　　B：你是說泰瑞嗎？

　　A：不，我是說派瑞。

7. A：我再重覆一次指示（或：我們再看一次指示）。

　　B：需要再看一次嗎？

　　A：是的，以免有人不懂，或沒聽到提示。

　　B：好的。

## 第 4 章

1. A：(i)我不確定我是否聽懂，你能重覆一次嗎？

　　B：在下一個紅綠燈的地方左轉，直走到叉路的地方，然後轉到右邊，走過兩個街口一直到橋邊為止。(ii)這樣清楚了嗎？（或：你聽懂我說的嗎？）

　　A：嗯，你是說我走這條路可以到金門大橋？

　　B：沒錯，就照著我的指示走吧。

2. A：史密斯先生，謝謝你今天和我見面。

　　B：這是我的榮幸。

　　A：我想要問你關於上次訪問時你所說的一段話。

　　B：哦，是什麼？

　　A：你說過你永遠不會從政。(i)你是指在任何情況下，你都不會跨入政壇嗎？

　　B：嗯，當然，如果有機會的話，我不會放棄的。(ii)我所說的是我今年不會跨入政壇。

3. A：你是坐六點的車來的嗎？

　　B：不，我坐七點的車來的。

　　A：你確定嗎？我以為你說過是六點呢。

　　B：我是說過，不過我的計劃改了。

4. A： 參議員,有人引用你的話,說是「有錢人絕不要赴戰場。」

　　B： (i)他引用錯了,(ii)我所說的是「 人們永遠不該兵戎相見。」

## 第 5 章

1. A： 我要買一件藍色衣服。

　　B： 你喜歡哪一類型的衣服,能否請你說明確一點?

　　　　（ 你能不能多解釋一點？）

　　A： 你說的「類型」是指什麼?（什麼意思？）

　　B： 嗯,你是想要結婚用、上班用、還是宴會用的服裝?

　　A： 我懂了,我要買一件宴會服。

　　B： 請跟我來,我帶你到我們的宴會服部門。

2. A： 身為美國總統,我會消滅貧窮和犯罪。

　　B： 你能否細談一下你將如何做?（你能否詳細說明？）

　　A： 我很樂意。事實上,這裏有本小冊子,詳述我打擊貧窮、犯罪的計劃。

3. A： 那家美國公司正在這裏建一座新廠。

　　B： "plant"是指什麼?（"plant"是什麼意思？）（或："plant"？）

　　A： 是指工廠。

4. A： 中國人信奉各種不同的宗教。

　　B： 你能舉例嗎?（舉例來說？）（或:舉例說明？）（或:例如？）

　　A： 佛教,道教和基督教。

5. A： 你有看到那婦人的小孩嗎?

　　B： 沒有,怎樣?（你幹嘛問我這個？）

　　A： 那小孩有雙可愛的棕眼。

　　B： 哦,對,我現在看到了,真的很漂亮!

6. A： 你是什麼意思？

　B： 我是說（*我的意思是*）（*或：我是指*）在快樂的人身邊比較好。

　A： 你是說我不快樂囉？

　B： 不是！不過有些人是。

## 第*6*章

## PART I

1. A： 我們不能告訴瑪麗，那樣會傷了她的心。

　B： 太遲了。*老實告訴你吧*，我已經把整個實情告訴她了。

　A： 那她怎麼說？

　B： 她說她了解。

2. A： 孩子們可以用這個操場來練習嗎？

　B： 嗯，*按理說*，非本鎮居民是不准使用這個操場，但是付一點錢的話，
　　　則可以使用兩個小時。

3. A： 當前許多防治犯罪的文章指出死刑並不能遏止犯罪。

　B： 那不是絕對的。

　A： 你是什麼意思？

　B： *大致說來*，例如在德州，犯罪率就因死刑的成立而降低。

## PART II

1. A： 莎拉穿橘色的比穿藍色的好看。

　B： 我不同意，我覺得她穿什麼都好看。
　　　（*你的話多少有點道理，但是我覺得她穿什麼顏色都好看。*）

　A： 我不是說她穿藍的不好看。

　B： 嗯，我覺得她穿藍的也很好看。

2. A： 我覺得每個人都該結婚。

   B： 不，你錯了！有些人就是不喜歡一輩子跟「某個人」住在一起。

     （我懂你的意思，但是有些人不想一輩子和「某個人」生活在一起。）

   A： 嗯，我覺得養一個家是最重要的。


3. A： 氣象預報說：整個週末都會下雨。

   B： 我聽到的是說周末不會下雨。

   A： 我想你聽錯了。我一直在聽的氣象預報一向都很準。

     （哦，我不知道，但是我收聽的氣象報告一向很準確。）

   B： 你什麼時候聽到那則預報的？

   A： 這個星期一開始的時候。

   B： 嗯，我是幾分鐘前才聽到氣象預報的，我想這則<u>比較</u>正確吧！


# 第 7 章

## PART I

1. A： 先生，我要退回這個東西。

   B： 有什麼問題嗎？

   A： 這台錄放影機不能錄影。

   B： 嗯…噢…我，呃…

   A： 怎麼了？

   B： 恐怕…呃…這個保證期限已經過了。


2. A： 翠西，你是不是又忘記做功課了？

   B： 噢，是這樣的…呃…我…

   A： 忘了，還是沒忘？

   B： 是的，我忘記了。


3. A： 你要不要和喬及我一起去看戲？

   B： 噢，是…呃…我是想去…但是，呃…你知道…

   A： 好吧！也許改天好了。

4. A： 我認為約翰會是下任總統。

　　B： 你為什麼那樣說呢？

　　A： 呃，噢，是…我是指…你知道…

　　B： 你只是猜想而已？

　　A： 是啦！根據民意調查猜的啦！

　　B： 噢，我知道了。

## PART II

1. A： 我希望丹尼斯能說出他真正的感覺。

　　B： 你問過他嗎？

　　A： 沒有，他總是非常無禮。

　　B： 什麼？

　　A： 哦，我是指「他總會為自己辯護」。

　　B： 也許你應該老實地對他說，而他可能會老實地回答你。

2. A： 畢業典禮幾點開始？

　　B： 早上一點。

　　A： 早上一點？

　　B： 哦，對不起，我是指「下午」，下午一點。

## 第 8 章

1. A： 你知道嗎？（或：猜猜看。）

　　B： 什麼？

　　A： 我們將有位新老板，你知道是誰嗎？

　　B： 新老板是誰有什麼關係嗎？

　　A： 沒有，不過我希望事情會因為這個改變而有所好轉。

2. A： 你知道嗎？（或：猜猜看。）

　　B： 什麼？

　　A： 我明年要上大學了。

　　B： 哦，是嗎？你在那兒要做些什麼？

　　A： 我不清楚。

　　B： 慢慢想吧！別急著下決定。


3. A： 哇！佩姬是個漂亮的新娘。

　　B： 是啊！她看起來像個公主！

　　A： 告訴你們，（或：我告訴你們，）（或：這樣如何？）

　　　　我們何不和她合照一張？

　　B： 好主意！


4. A： 我認為我們該去加拿大渡假。

　　B： 這樣如何？（或：這聽起來怎樣？）

　　A： 什麼？

　　B： 你覺得也去阿拉斯加好不好？阿拉斯加鄰近加拿大。

　　A： 好主意！我們就去阿拉斯加和加拿大。


5. A： 這樣如何？（或：這聽起來怎樣？）（或：你覺得這樣如何？）

　　　　我們在舞會中要放爵士樂。

　　B： 我不喜歡那個主意。

　　A： 為什麼不喜歡呢？

　　B： 因為爵士舞很難跳。

　　A： 那麼，我知道該怎麼做了。（或：這樣如何？）當天晚上我們先放爵

　　　　士，再放搖滾。

　　B： 我不曉得，我比較喜歡只有一種音樂。

6. A： 你要出去嗎？

   B： 對。

   A： 你要去哪？

   B： 去超級市場。

   A： 順帶一提，你到了那兒，能不能買些橘子汁？

7. A： 你今天要參加世界和平展示會嗎？

   B： 我不知道，我還是不大舒服，你有沒有止頭痛的藥？

   A： 我沒有。不過無論如何，我希望能在那兒看到你。

## 第9章

1. A： 我真等不及要看這場表演了，去年…

   B： 容我打個岔，能否請你們移過去兩個位子？你們坐在我們的位子上。

   A： 哦，很抱歉。

2. A： 我來自紐約，…

   B： 抱歉，我忍不住聽了你的話。你是否說你來自紐約？

   A： 對，沒錯，你也來自紐約嗎？

3. A： 在約會六年以後，布魯斯和泰咪結婚了…

   B： 等等！我不知道吔！

   A： 我也是接到他們的明信片才知道的。

4. A： 我很高興能到這所大學來，其學術水準是全美最高的。

   B： 抱歉，鮑伯，我能問你一個問題嗎？（或：我能說些什麼嗎？）

   A： 當然，請說。

5. A： 路易斯安那州的東南部遭佛羅倫斯颶風侵襲。

   B： 抱歉，為什麼取名為"佛羅倫斯"？

   A： 不知道，而且為什麼是女孩子的名字？

6. A： 朵麗思要去美國，而且…

　　B： 慢著，湯姆，你是說朵麗思？

　　A： 是啊，她明天就要離開了，你不知道嗎？


# 第 *10* 章
## PART I

1. 德國境內有一架飛機失事了！

　(a) （重覆）　德國有一架飛機失事了？！

　(b) （附和）　真的嗎？

　(c) （驚訝）　哦，我的天呀！好可怕！

　(d) （同情）　噢，聽到這個消息真難過。


2. 滑雪的計畫取消了！

　(a) （重覆）　取消了？！（或：哦！不要！）

　(b) （氣餒）　真失望！

　(c) （憤怒）　哦，真可惡！

　(d) （其他）　太可惜了！


3. 鮑伯和珍要結婚了！

　(a) （重覆）　他們要結婚了？！

　(b) （驚訝）　你在開玩笑！

　(c) （高興）　太棒了！我真為他們高興。

　(d) （其他）　哦，是嗎？什麼時候？


4. 約翰將會是美國下一任總統！

　(a) （重覆）　約翰將是下一任總統？！

　(b) （附加）　哦，是嗎？

　(c) （不關心）　那又怎樣？

　(d) （補充）　那麼，威廉將是下一任副總統！

## PART II

1. A：我認為鮑伯很帥。

   B：他有沒有覺得妳也很有魅力？

   A：我不知道，但毫無置疑地，他很吸引我。

   B：我要說的是，妳已爲他瘋狂了。


2. A：我想打電話給我爸媽，但是長途電話費太貴了。

   B：你何不用寫信的方式呢？

   A：那是個好主意！他們一定很高興收到我的信！

   B：而且最重要的是，你可以省下一筆錢！


# 第 11 章

1. 能再看到你實在太棒了。

   A：能再看到你真好！

   B：我也是。

   A：請跟我保持連絡，好朋友是不容易交到的。

   B：我會的，你也要跟我聯繫。

   A：保重。


2. 我的電話費會太高了，我最好掛電話。

   A：電話費要超支了，我得掛電話了！

   B：我忘了你打的是長途電話，我不再跟你多說了。

   A：和你講電話真好。

   B：我也很高興和你談話。

   A：我會想你的，再見。

   B：再見囉！

3. 抱歉佔用你這麼多時間，我最好講到這裏。

    Ａ：抱歉佔用你這麼多時間，我最好講到這裏。

    Ｂ：和你聊天很愉快。

    Ａ：我會再打電話給你的。

    Ｂ：好的，我也會打電話給你。

    Ａ：再見。

    Ｂ：再見。


4. 有空聚聚。

    Ａ：我們有空再聚聚吧！

    Ｂ：好啊！

    Ａ：嗯，我很快會再打電話給你。

    Ｂ：好的，不用急。

    Ａ：晚安。

    Ｂ：晚安。

心得筆記欄

||||||||||||| ● 學習出版公司門市部 ● |||||||||||||||

台北地區：台北市許昌街 10 號 2 樓 TEL：(02)3314060・3319209
台中地區：台中市綠川東街 32 號 8 樓 23 室
　　　　　TEL：(04)2232838

|||||||||||||||||||||||||||||||||||||||||||

# 英語 12 招行遍天下

編　　著／陳 美 黛
發 行 所／學習出版有限公司　　　☎ (02) 7045525
郵 撥 帳 號／0512727-2 學習出版社帳戶
登 記 證／局版台業 2179 號
印 刷 所／裕強彩色印刷有限公司
台 北 門 市／台北市許昌街 10 號 2 F　　☎ (02) 3314060・3319209
台 中 門 市／台中市綠川東街 32 號 8 F 23 室　☎ (04) 2232838
台灣總經銷／學英文化事業公司　　　☎ (02) 2187307
美國總經銷／Evergreen Book Store　☎ (818) 2813622

售價：新台幣一百五十元正
1997 年 11 月 1 日一版三刷